Relationship Building and Transforming:
The Levels of Platonic and Erotic Love

Relationship Building and Transforming: The Levels of Platonic and Erotic Love

By Terence T. Gorski

An Edited Transcription of a Workshop
at the Fashion Institute of Technology
New York City

Based on the CENAPS Model of Treatment

Herald House/Independence Press
3225 South Noland Road
P.O. Box 1770
Independence, MO 64055-0770

1-800-767-8181
816-252-5010

Published by
Herald House/Independence Press
3225 South Noland Road
P.O. Box 1770
Independence, MO 64055-0770

Printed in the United States of America

ISBN 0-8309-0638-X

97 96 95 94 93 1 2 3 4 5

Introduction

A relationship is the contract between two human beings who choose to be partners and to love one another. Most of us want to be in a healthy, loving, caring relationship with another person, but many of us do not have a clue as to how to do this. The following pages will define relationships even further, examine their potential, and offer some basic relationship-building skills as a guide.

I never set out to become an expert on relationships. My involvement with relationships came about as a result of my training as an alcoholism and drug abuse counselor. I began specializing in the treatment of relapse-prone alcoholics—alcoholics who cannot stay sober no matter how hard they try. I found that many people who are recovering from chemical dependency end up relapsing as a result of a dysfunctional relationship that crashes and burns. When this happens, they go out and get drunk over it. As part of my work I developed a model for understanding relationships that can be quickly taught to recovering people. It's a series of guidelines they can use to stay out of the crazy kinds of relationships that destroy the quality of sobriety. Yet it also allows them an opportunity to get into and build healthy relationships or to transform their present relationships.

Then, a number of years ago, an interesting thing happened. An associate of mine called to see if I'd do a presentation on "Intimacy in Recovery." I told her that I don't do intimacy: I do relapse prevention; I do diagnosis; I do group therapy. She thought it was a good idea anyway, so she put me down on the program and, after sending out 35,000 brochures, informed me by letter that I was giving the keynote lecture. So with a tad of resentment, I flew off to San Diego, did a forty-five-minute lecture on addictive relationships, healthy relationships, and how to get from here to there. I returned to Chicago and back to my obsession with relapse prevention.

About a year later I got a call from an ACOA group in San Diego that wanted me to do my talk on "Intimacy in Recovery" at its first national meeting. That talk was also recorded and spread rapidly through the recovering community, not only in the United States but also in Canada and Europe.

From there I started getting calls to do workshops and lectures, and I now spend about one-third of my time lecturing or writing about relationships and intimacy. This has led to writing a book called *Getting Love Right: Learning the Choices of Healthy Intimacy,* to be published by Simon & Schuster in 1993. I was also invited to host a three-part Public Broadcasting System (PBS) Series produced by KBDI in Denver which was nationally syndicated in 1992 to PBS stations around the country. The videotapes of those programs are available from Herald House/Independence Press (1-800-767-8181).

The success of these ideas tells me that I must be saying something that other people find helpful. So I'm going to share my current thinking on relationships and hope you find it useful.

Terence T. Gorski

The Relationship Snake

I want to start out by telling you the story of the snake. Many of you have heard it, but it's a story that is worth repeating.

There once was a man who, while walking through the woods on a cold winter's day, found a poisonous snake frozen in the middle of a path. At first he was startled and began to run away, but then he looked at the poor frozen thing. It was so pretty and so helpless. "And it needs me," he thought. "Without me, this snake will die an ugly death."

So the man picked up the snake and carried it home, knowing that rapidly thawing out cold-blooded creatures would bring them back to life. He built a big fire and took the pillows off his own bed and placed them in front of the fireplace. He laid the snake in front of the pillows, went into the kitchen, and warmed a bowl of hot milk for the snake when it awoke. Then he sat there with eager anticipation as he watched the snake come back to life. The snake wiggled a little bit, and as he went to give it the bowl of milk, the snake lashed out and bit him, injecting a lethal dose of venom in his arm.

He felt the heat of that poison rushing up the veins of his arm, back to his heart, and he knew he had only a few seconds to live. He looked at the snake and said, "Snake, how could you do this to me? After all that I've done for you, how could you kill me like this? I picked you up in the woods and brought you into my home. I took the pillows off my bed. I built a fire, thawed you out, and fixed you milk. I saved your life and now you kill me. It's all your fault."

The snake looked at him and said, "Hey buddy, stop your whining. It's not my fault that you're dying. It's not my fault that I bit you. You knew that I was a poisonous snake when you picked me up. What did you expect me to do? Give you a kiss?"

This story draws a parallel to many dysfunctional relationships. We pick up a poisonous snake, get bitten, and swear off, saying, "Never again, no more relationships." We abstain for a while until we become lonely and desperate. We crave affection, gender affirmation, and we start getting real antsy and itchy, desperate and vulnerable. Suddenly, we're back in. We see another snake and feel we must pick it up.

Society's View

If I had to identify the single reason why so many people in the United States are involved in dysfunctional relationships over and over again, I'd say this: *We receive more training in how to drive a car than we do in how to conduct an intimate relationship or how to parent a child.* And when parents, who don't understand how to be intimate, raise children, they raise children who don't understand how to be intimate. This is a society-wide problem in America today.

The entire parenting structure of the nation changed with the Baby Boom generation. Before this generation, people were parented by living, breathing human beings. During the 1950s, our primary parenting was transferred to an electronic device called the television. We learned our images of love, marriage, family, intimacy, and caring from the television set. As a matter of fact, most of us spent five times as much time interacting with the TV than we did with any adult.

When I was a kid, I sat hypnotized by that one-eyed monster. Programmed into my brain was "Ozzie & Harriet," "Leave It to Beaver," and the societal ideal of the perfect family. There were no problems, and all of the struggles were relatively benign. There were no alcoholics, no pubescent teenagers, no financial setbacks. There were good kids and bad kids. Eddie Haskell was a bad kid, and you clearly knew it. Television presented the image of the sterilized American family which no family could actually live up to.

Then, of course, as I moved into adolescence, the Beaver started to bore me. So I got involved in other entertainment media that presented a polar opposite. I was fascinated with James Bond, especially when *Dr. No* came out. I liked the fact that this guy could have these wonderful, intensely intimate relationships with women without ever having a feeling. Intense sexuality, no emotion. Shoot him out of the air, and he ends up making love in the life raft. It's absolutely wonderful! And we have a whole series of heroes like this. They get their arm blown off with a 45 magnum, and they're having hot sex with their girlfriend that night. What real men!

These types of fantasy images have given us unrealistic expectations of relationships. Most people have a very distorted or confused notion of what a relationship is and what a relationship is capable of doing for us.

A New Vision of Relationships

I have a new vision of what relationships can be and what they are designed to be. My primary mission is to comfort the disturbed and to disturb the comfortable.

Many people are already disturbed, saying that relationships aren't working the way they should or that they don't match the societal standard or norm. They get bored periodically with their partner. They get into conflicts. The sex isn't that great anymore, and they know that there is something wrong somewhere. And yes, there is. They are not crazy for being disturbed, but there are things they can do about it. Many people are very smugly comfortable, though. They know exactly what a relationship is, what it should be, and how it should operate. In their minds, the only problem is that no one else shares their vision of the ultimately healthy relationship.

In a singles workshop a while ago, I put all of the men on one side of the room and all of the women on the other side. Then I told them to get together in groups of six to ten people to discuss the primary reason why they were not able to get into a healthy relationship at this time in their lives. Most of the men and women arrived at the same conclusion: "I am a high-quality person, but I can't find a high-quality partner who is healthy enough to relate to me!" We had a whole roomful of people—150 men and women—who, in their own minds, felt that they were high-quality partners. Adrift in a sea of people who were not able to meet their needs, they thought their only problem was to learn how to find the perfect partner. The trouble was, *no one* met their standards.

If you feel you are so healthy that there are no partners who can meet your standards, you have a problem. If you have unrealistically high expectations of potential partners, refuse to change your standards, and become involved with fallible human beings, then you are going to get very lonely.

The Myth of the Perfect Partner

Most Americans believe in the myth of the perfect partner. They believe there is someone out there somewhere who can meet all their needs. This myth has destroyed many people's ability to be intimate. In reality, *there is no such thing as a perfect relationship or perfect partner.* And searching for it can be a major obstacle to learning how to get love right.

When we look for a perfect partner, we look for somebody who is going to magically fix us, somebody who will somehow make us feel complete, transforming us into someone that we're not. And we know that if we can just find that person, everything will be all right.

> The myth of the perfect partner
> can destroy the chances
> of building a healthy, intimate relationship.

This "perfect partner" concept is developed early in childhood. It's seen in fairy tales, literature, song lyrics, television, and movies and taught to us by previous generations. You'll also see, later on, that when a relationship fails and we see our partner realistically, he or she uncannily reminds us of our parents.

To develop a healthy, effective, meaningful relationship, you must put an end to the perfect myth and accept that there is no perfect partner. All partners are people and all people are fallible human beings. Although we are more compatible with some people than others, no one will perfectly meet all of our needs.

Most of us, however, are powerfully attracted to a certain type of person. We don't understand why, but some people "turn us on" and other people don't. When we meet someone who turns us on there is the tendency to believe that we have found THE ONE, him or her, Mr.

or Ms. Right. When we meet that person something powerful kicks up inside of us. Our eyes lock across the room and we instantly know this is our soul mate for all eternity. We have karma together. We have shared past experiences that are just screaming out to be resolved in the here and now. This time we're going to make it! This person is going to fill me up and make me feel whole and complete. Turtle doves will fly overhead and the universe will be healthy and whole.

When you see someone who causes this reaction in you, I recommend that you turn around and run the other way! Why? Because you probably know exactly where the relationship is going to go. What should you do instead? Find the most boring person at the party, walk up to him or her, and start dating.

I don't mean that you literally should date boring beings. What I mean is that you should avoid dating the same type of person that you have always dated. You should avoid getting involved with the same snake over and over again and then wondering why you keep getting bit.

Addictive Relationships

There are two kinds of dysfunctional relationships. The first is the addictive, compulsive, or driven relationship; the second is the apathetic, dull, or boring relationship.

Types of Dysfunctional Relationships

1. Compulsive
2. Apathetic

An addictive relationship is the type of relationship that is built on intensity without substance. You meet someone and the firecrackers go off, the bells chime, and the whistles blow. You are infatuated beyond belief. Then you act on your infatuation by getting involved with the person. You have hot sex with him or her, and when you wake up the next morning and try to carry on a conversation, you find that there's no substance. You ask yourself, "How did I do this? How could I have found this person attractive?"

Sometimes it takes months to find out there's no substance there because the sexual attraction is so strong. So if we're going to define addictive or compulsive relationships, they're relationships where the primary feature is emotional and sexual intensity but with very little substance to back it up.

Apathetic Relationships

There's another form of the dysfunctional relationship—the apathetic relationship. They occur when you find someone you don't feel attracted to and don't really value. As a result, this person doesn't have the power to hurt you. You get into a sterile, safe relationship. Apathetic relationships are safe, but they lack intimacy and a deep sense of connectedness. These apathetic relationships are just as destructive as addictive relationships, although in a different way. Where addictive relationships explode, apathetic relationships fizzle out. Neither one meets your needs.

Intensity and Substance

There was a major study done in the late 1960s of married people who had successful intimate relationships. This group reported that they were subjectively satisfied with the relationship after twenty years. They said they were basically happy and content and that the relationship met their needs. They would even marry their partner all over again if given the opportunity.

The study found one thing that made absolutely no difference to the long-term success of an intimate relationship: the intensity of the passion at the beginning of the relationship. Some people reported very intense passionate love at first sight. Others said they felt nothing when they met and slowly the passion built over time.

Intensity has nothing to do with the long-term prognosis of a relationship. It has a lot to do with the short-term, here-and-now gratification. And if what you're after is a mind-blowing experience *tonight*, go after intensity as your sole criteria. Evaluate the whole thing by the number of sex hormones released when you gaze into the eyes or at the other bodily parts of your partner. If those hormones start to flow, your heart starts beating, and you get extremely, intensely, passionately attracted, recognize it for what it is.

If, by accident, you happen to feel that way toward someone with whom you share substance, the relationship will work very well. But there's no correlation between the intensity of passion and whether or not you share substantial values. Many times we are intensely attracted to people with whom we have little or nothing in common.

Substance is the foundation of long-term intimacy. There are three elements that create substance in a relationship: shared values, goals, and life-style preferences.

Substance is based on shared...

1. Values
2. Goals
3. Life-style Preferences

Values

The first element of substance that showed up in every study of long-term, successful marriage is shared values. *A value is a standard in which we are willing to invest time, energy, and resources to acquire and maintain.* Everybody centers their life around a primary central value, a basic organizing value. It's different for each person. For example, the basic organizing value in my life is the contribution that I make to the world professionally. It's not a matter of good or bad. It's simply how I choose to live my life. And around that central value, I build love relationships, friends, recreations, and so on.

Suppose I met somebody whose primary central organizing value was to raise a family and to have a man who comes home at five o'clock every night, who shares coequal roles in the household responsibilities, who becomes a coequal father, and who wants to live out west on a farm with a babbling brook in front of it. And what if this person felt that a job's only value is to earn enough money to live off of and to keep the homestead going. I wouldn't be a very good match for someone like that.

In my early twenties, I was deeply involved with a woman who had that value system, and she was wise enough to realize that it wouldn't work, so she ended the relationship with me. If I had tried to bend myself out of shape to accommodate her value system, we would have ended up breaking apart because we didn't share a common core value. As a result, the essence of who I am could not be shared and experienced in that relationship. The type of woman who is going to enjoy a relationship with me, and me with her, is somebody who shares the same work ethic, somebody who has the same central values.

Goals

The second area of substance in a relationship is shared goals. You've got to know where you're going in life if you want to have an effective relationship. Human beings are goal-setting creatures. We're meaning-seeking souls. We want to know what we're doing and where we're going. I don't believe that there is an ultimate, inherent meaning in life. The meaning in life is what we put on it. When in a relationship, two people work together to assign meaning and purpose to their lives. Once we decide what our life and our relationship means, we need to know where we are going from there. This is the problem with relationships. They always go somewhere because life always goes somewhere. Life is a process. It is a movement and a growth. You can't stand still, you have to go somewhere and do something.

> The problem with relationships
> is that they always go somewhere.
> This is because life always goes somewhere
> and relationships are a part of life.

I want to share with you a new vision of relationship as partnership, not relationship as orgasm. This is a new perspective for many people. Why? Because many of us were trained by the media to sexualize everything we look at, to view everything as a sexual object, and to tap into that sexual energy. The primary basis of a relationship is partnership. In a healthy, functional relationship, sexuality represents about 10 percent of the relationship. The only time it takes a greater dimension is in the early stages of a relationship and when the sex isn't working well for one or both partners. When your sex life becomes incompatible, then sexuality grows to consume 90 percent of the relationship. If you've got a healthy, functional sex life and your sex, intimacy, and affection needs are being met, sex falls into the background of the relationship and partnership comes to the forefront.

A conscious relationship is the ideal, not an unconscious one. In a conscious relationship, both partners know their values and goals. And they know their partner well enough to assure that their values and goals are compatible. They know their goals and they know that they're pulling in the same direction.

Life-style Preferences

The third area of substance is common life-style preferences—the way you want to live on a day-to-day intimate basis. If you're married or living with someone, you're in a committed relationship. The difference between this and a dating relationship or love affair is the sharing of a living space in a primary intimate way. You're sharing bathrooms. You're waking up in the morning and seeing what the person looks like. You're dealing with each other's dirty laundry. Somebody has got to take out the garbage, and somebody has got to do the dishes. You're on top of one another. If you clutter, your partner pays the price.

I don't understand why but "clutterers" are attracted to "neatniks." It seems to be a universal rule. And it's a universal problem where the neatnik suffers first because there are different levels of clutter tolerance. The clutterer can stand the world being a mess and the neatnik can't. The clutterer never understands this and feels if the mess bothers you, you should clean it up. The neatnik feels that's unfair simply because it is unfair, and you now have the basis of one of the most common problems in a relationship.

Most of the people in marriage counseling who are really committed to each other are not dealing with huge life-crushing things that are destroying their marriages. It's all the little life-style preferences. He won't clean up the kitchen or she won't do the laundry. It's important to find someone who shares a similar standard of life-style as you do, who wants to live in a similar environment in a similar way. Then a lot of this is going to harmonize.

There's a mistaken belief that if you're in an intimate relationship, it requires constant work. A dysfunctional relationship, where you can't be yourself, requires constant work. Because if you can't be you, you're constantly adjusting yourself to accommodate your partner or forcing your partner to adjust to accommodate you. So you have to work, struggle, change, negotiate, and compromise all the time because when you are exactly the way you want to be, your partner doesn't like you. And when your partner is exactly the way they want to be, you don't like them. And this is called incompatibility.

Intensity without Substance

I'm going to share with you a basic truth. You can have really hot sex with an incompatible partner. It's intensity without substance. It's high-intensity sex minus common values, goals, and life-style preferences. The sex is great, but you're going in different directions in life, trying to accomplish different things. You want to live on a day-to-day basis in accordance with one standard and your partner wants to live in accordance with another. You're constantly negotiating, struggling, and working with the whole thing.

If addictive relationships are going to continue, both partners must become obsessive, compulsive, and driven. Because when incompatibilities exist in values, goals, and life-style preferences, you have to focus on the intensity, and you must keep it there all the time. Once the intensity diminishes, you confront the reality of the incompatibility.

When relationships become obsessive, we think about them all the time. We obsess about them. We think about the relationship when we should be thinking about other things—like working. They are compulsive. We feel this irrational urge to be with our partner all the time. We can't let them go. We can't let them out of our sight. When we're with them we've got to touch them, hold on to them, take their hand, hug them, kiss them, make love to them. Even when we're in restaurants. Then we don't understand when the person wants to be left alone and starts pushing us away. Addictive relationships are also driven. We feel we don't have a choice about this. There's something inside of us that's driving us.

I'm going to suggest to you that healthy love is not driven love. Healthy love is love where there is choice. You don't *have to be* in a healthy relationship, you *want to be.* Or you can choose not to be. You know beyond a doubt that if your partner comes after you with a hot ice pick one night, trying to stab your eyes out, you will leave.

> Healthy love is not driven love.
> With healthy love we have choices!

A man in a driven relationship called me and said that he was really in love with this woman, but there was a slight problem. She had tried to stab him with a kitchen knife the previous night while he was asleep. She slashed his arms, and he had to go to the emergency room. What should he do? I asked him his plans, and he said that he was going to sleep in the same room with her tonight, but that he was going to set the clock to wake him up every hour so he would be vigilant and be able to protect himself from another attack. When I asked him why he was going to do that, he replied that he really loved her. He cared about her, and he needed her. That is not a choice, that's a drive. There's a big difference between being driven and having choices. Healthy intimacy is about becoming a healthy, intimate choice-maker by breaking free of addictively driven relationships.

I am convinced that most people who are in driven relationships are not *in love* with their partner, they are *in need* of their partner. They confuse the feeling of love, which they have never known, with a feeling called emotional hunger.

An emotional hunger is something that most people develop as children when they don't get the love, caring, and nurturing that they needed from their parents. It results in this feeling of primal emptiness. We're empty at the core of our being. We don't feel whole or complete. We feel like there is something missing in us and believe there is nothing we can do to fill ourselves up. We look to a magical lover as the one person in the whole universe who has the power to fill us up. This one and only lover, destined from all time and eternity, will be the key that fits our lock.

The mythology of the one and only is very deadly. Imagine going to a party and you're cruising the crowd and socializing. All of a sudden, there he or she is. You experience that surge, just looking at him or her. You feel whole and complete for the first time in your life. Or at least since the last time this happened. This individual whose name you don't even know, is now in your mind: the one and only. It has happened. It is love at first sight. You know, beyond a doubt, that this is it. There is no one else in the whole world for you.

This puts enormous pressure on you. You've found the only person in the whole universe who can fix you, who can make you feel good. Now what if you screw this up? What if you blow it?

Suddenly, your insecurities arise and you start putting yourself down. What if this person finds out how desperate, needy, and inadequate you truly are. You just know that he or she is not going to love the real you, so you better get on your best behavior and become something you're actually not. You present the best side of yourself to this person, hiding everything you don't want them to see, so he or she will fall in love with you.

So you've got two people falling in love with the image they have of each other. Notice this, you fall in love with the image, not the real person. And that works out well if you only see each other on Friday and Saturday nights. But as you get into a more intimate relationship, and you start living together or you get married, the other person suddenly changes. When you observe your partner in their natural habitat, you now see who the partner really is and you're shocked. But that's all right because your partner is shocked also.

And now the relationship moves into its second stage where the power struggle ensues. You are going to make this person, for his or her own good, be what they need to be to make this relationship work. It's your mission to change them. But that's all right because they're trying to change you, too.

Now you're locked into a hideous power struggle that will have one of three outcomes. In the most common outcome, the relationship blows apart. People separate, realizing they goofed. There is still a "one and only" out there, you just haven't found the right one. In time, you go out looking again and the same thing happens.

The other alternative is settling. You settle for the fact that this relationship will never be able to meet your needs and will never really let you be happy. But you rationalize that your partner is a little better than any other partner you might find. And although he or she is really pretty bad, it's not terrible, so you'll accept her the way she is. You become a martyr, suffering while performing your duties and obligations, awaiting your reward in the next life. You feel it's worth the trade-off.

You get what you settle for!

With the third alternative, which is the least common, you recognize what's really going on. You decide that if you're going to have a happy, healthy, functional relationship, you will have to take a look at what it is inside of you that drives you to need this person to be a certain way. And you ask: What can I do to fill myself up? What can I do to make myself whole and complete? What can I do to resolve the issues in me that are preventing me from loving and feeling really intimate about another human being?

First the Self

Before we look at the possibility of healthy love, we need to acknowledge the self as the primary principle. And we start by reclaiming who we are as a human being. We need to get honest with ourselves and to work on our unfinished issues. Then we have the possibility of sharing ourselves with another human being in an intimate way. We can stop being obsessive because the obsession focuses on the partner instead of the self. We can stop being compulsive because the compulsive drive is for the partner to fill you up and fix you. As a result, we can stop being driven in our relationship styles and habits.

Addictive relationships are very attractive because they have the power that drugs have. When you take a drug, the way you think changes automatically, especially if you're an addict. If you want to think better, take a drug. If you want to feel better, take a drug. If you want to act better, take a drug. It won't really be better, but you won't notice that reality.

How We Think

Addictive relationships have the power to change how we think, feel, and act. This is why they're so appealing. The addictive relationship turns off our minds and allows us to stop thinking. The intensity of the addictive relationship turns off our mental capacity. We stop thinking and turn into a blithering idiot. This phenomenon is easy to observe objectively in our friends. They fall in love and their mental capacity totally goes. They can't even observe, realistically, who their partner is.

A woman I worked with had the tendency to get into addictive relationships. She came in the office one day, totally infatuated, glazed in the eyes, bursting to tell me about the new "him." She said he was a wonderful guy, absolutely romantic, sensitive, warm, caring.

I asked her where she had met him. "At the gas station," she said. "He was riding a Harley in this really cool black leather jacket with studs on it." A really hot guy, shirt open, hair on his chest, just a hot guy.

I asked her to tell me more. She said they went out, had coffee, and went to her place. They had great sex. She was in love with Charlie. I asked her what his last name was and she didn't know. I asked what he did for a living and she hadn't asked. She just knew he wasn't married, even though she didn't ask that either. He promised to call her that night, but he never did. And she couldn't understand why. He was such a warm, caring, concerned, compassionate human being.

When sex hormones kick in, the brain turns off. We're trained to do it societally. We are told, "Love doesn't make sense." So many people are involved in irrational, destructive, and senseless love relationships that we justify by saying "Love is crazy."

I'm going to share with you another basic truth. *Crazy love is crazy; healthy love is not. Healthy love is eminently sensible.* You don't spend a lot of time thinking about it, and you don't have to turn off your mind. You can still think rationally about yourself, about your partner, about the relationship and about other aspects of your life. You don't have to stop thinking as a condition of the relationship.

People in an addictive relationship turn off their minds very easily. Quite often, it's a protective reflex from childhood. They turned off their minds to survive growing up in a dysfunctional home.

How We Feel

Addictive relationships also change how we feel. They produce a powerful euphoria that distorts our other feelings. This passion, this intensity, this infatuation is so strong, so powerful, that it blocks out any other feeling we have. If we're depressed, it overrides the depression. If we're angry, it surpasses the anger. No matter what we're feeling when we are with our partner, we psych ourselves into this state of infatuation.

We also adhere to a fundamental societal value where people disown responsibility for their sexuality: "You make me feel this way." "She turns me on." "He does it to me." When we do this, we are not responsible for our sexual feelings and actions.

Here's a concept that sounds really crazy. You don't turn me on. I turn myself on to you. Many people have never recognized that if I get sexually turned on, it's because I turn me on, not you. I turn myself on by the way I think, the way I image, imagine, and fantasize. I turn me on to you.

> You don't turn me on.
> I turn myself on to you.

There is no one-and-only partner who's going to turn me on. The bell-shaped curve from basic statistics says that out of all the men and women you meet, probably one-third have the potential to be a meaningful love partner for you.

Now you may do things that make it easier for me to turn myself on, that invite the turn on. You may flirt with me. You may, through no decision of yours, match a profile that I find very sexually attractive. It's easier for me to turn myself on to some people than to others. But I do it to me. You don't. The converse is also true. If I can turn myself on to you, I can also turn myself off. This is important to know if you are ever strongly attracted to a dangerous partner.

Infatuation

When I turn myself on to you, this turn-on state is called infatuation. I define infatuation as a state of temporary insanity marked by both euphoria and irrationality. The euphoria makes us feel high, and it creates an intense, passionate, highly pleasurable emotional state. Our entire brain chemistry changes as if we took a euphoric drug.

The irrationality occurs because our brain is turned off, and we can't think realistically about our partners, ourselves, or the relationship. When we become infatuated, our life becomes irrelevant, and we can't sanely see how the relationship fits into the bigger picture of our life.

The new love relationship becomes our absolute number-one priority, our spiritual center. Our primary organizing value is the relationship. Everything else drops to a very remote second place. We abandon long-term friends. We're willing to take risks with our jobs and our lives. It's insanity.

It is however, a lot of fun. It's reinforcing in the short run, but it can be problematic in the long run. So when you are infatuated, recognize it for what it is. See it as a state of temporary insanity that will pass. *Never make serious commitments while infatuated.* Don't start living with somebody or marry somebody. Don't give somebody your money or the keys to your apartment while the infatuation is intense. When you are infatuated, you don't have a clear picture of the person or the situation.

When you are infatuated, introduce your love partner to all of your friends. And then privately ask them what they think of him or her. If the thought of doing this terrifies you, I suggest there's something going on that you don't want to look at in this relationship. There's something underneath the infatuation.

> Infatuation is a state of temporary insanity marked by both euphoria and irrationality.

If your friends say, what a klutz, what a clod, he or she treats you badly, you'd better listen because your friends care about you. And you'd better enjoy this for what it is, see where it's going, and be cautious. You won't see the reality until the infatuation breaks.

Changing How We Act

Addictive relationships also have the power to change how we act and behave. The relationship gives us permission to try new and different behaviors. And we may say it's not our fault, that we've changed and it's your fault.

I worked with one couple where the guy was insanely jealous and tended to get violent. The woman involved was so in love with the man that she couldn't set boundaries. She refused to consider leaving him. When I finally got the communication going, the guy actually looked at her and said, "Sue, you've got to understand that before I met you, I felt like a little pile of garbage in the corner of a very large auditorium. And when I met you, I could find my self-esteem. I could find my self-worth. Because of you, I became somebody for the first time in my life. You did it for me."

That's so positively reinforcing. Imagine moving into someone's life and saving them from the depths of depression, fear, and everything else. Now, Sue perked up and said, "John, I just love you so much. Thank you for saying that."

Let's go one step further and look at the dark side of this. He was saying to her nonverbally, "Now, Sue, you've got to understand. If you ever leave me, I'm going to go back to being that little pile of garbage. And I just can't let that happen. If you try to leave me, I won't let you." Psychologically, they are now in a relationship where one partner needs the other, to be okay. It's like you have become my right arm and I need you there.

Now if you were walking down the street and someone comes at you with a chain saw and tries to cut off your arm, you have a right to get angry at him. You have a right to push him away. If he keeps coming at you, you have a right to him kick him, beat on him, and kill him. He's trying to cut off your arm so any action is self-defense. When you become someone's emotional right arm, and this person needs you to feel okay, he or she is going to get violent if you ever decide to leave. It's not because they love you but because they need you to fill up their emotional hunger.

If you are involved in an obsessive relationship where you or your partner acts out violently, I suggest you read a book by Susan Forward called *Obsessive Love.* Violence in a love relationship is very dangerous, and you need to separate from it and get professional help.

Shifting Responsibilities

All of this leads to a shift in responsibilities. Positive changes are attributed to the relationship. "Because of you, I am this way!" Negative changes tend to be blamed on the self. "If I were a better partner, if I would work harder, if I would just do it differently, things would be all right!"

Typically, you have one partner who attributes all the positive changes to the other partner. "You're doing everything right and I'm doing everything wrong." And then other partners quite often believe that they do everything right and you do everything wrong. Anytime there's a problem, this balance proves that you're not okay and they are. You're a very codependent person who's the doormat in the relationship. Your partner is the counterdependent, the borderline psychopath type of person who controls everything. He or she is always right and everything is your fault. There is a one-up, one-down dynamic of codependent and counterdependent.

Thinking Clearly

Healthy relationships are not a substitute for thinking clearly. In a healthy relationship, we are allowed to think clearly about who we are and who our partner is. We can clearly acknowledge our strengths and weaknesses. And if asked, we're able to describe and accept our partner's strengths and weaknesses. These weaknesses are of such a nature that they don't really bother us. They're not that big a deal, and it doesn't make that much difference if the partner chooses to change them.

This acceptance is not a substitute for thinking clearly about who I am. I can see myself—my strengths and my weaknesses. It's all right for me to change and learn and grow. My partner was not invested in me staying the way I am for all eternity. My partner wants what's best for me, and he or she is willing to allow me the freedom to grow and change.

There is a thing called incompatibility that occurs when people don't share common values, goals, and life-style preferences and they're not willing to change. They honor themselves enough not to sell out simply to have that partner. It's nobody's fault. It simply happens sometimes. When it becomes evident that there are irreconcilable incompatibilities and partners don't choose to be together, you don't have to work yourself into vengeful rages. You can disconnect and negotiate the end of a relationship or you can uncouple without violence, hate, and enduring long-term grief. You *can* work it out.

Coping with Our Feelings

A healthy relationship is not a substitute for coping with our feelings. In a healthy relationship, we don't psych ourselves into an infatuated frenzy to avoid dealing with depression, anger, sadness, or jealousy. In healthy relationships, we are able to know what we're feeling. We can communicate that to our partners, and they are able to listen to us and to understand and affirm our right to have our feelings. They're willing to deal with us in an honest way in the here and now about our emotional experiences. Of course, to have this understanding, we have to be able to do this with our partners as well.

Acting Responsibly

Healthy relationships are not a substitute for acting responsibly. Healthy partners do not tolerate irresponsible behaviors in their partners. When I am in a relationship, and my partner starts acting in an irresponsible way, I declare a crisis. I identify the irresponsible behavior. This behavior produces negative consequences to the relationship, to me, and to other people. I will not be a party to it. It's scary when you're married because you're legally responsible for the consequences of your partner. So we have to set limits. It's not okay for you to use the little piece of plastic to the point where I can go to jail for it.

Now, if you have two partners who value responsibility, it will work out okay. You become a positive check and balance to each other. Maybe you are not acting irresponsibly when I think you are, so we have to talk about this. Maybe through our dialogue process, I'll find out I was wrong.

People who love each other do not totally detach and let their partner go down the tubes without making a reasonable effort to intervene. It doesn't mean you destroy yourself to save your partner, but you make a reasonable effort to intervene.

In addictive relationships, we don't love our partner, we love how our partner makes us feel. And there's a very big difference between the two. If I love you, I want to see you do what is right for you even if it deprives me in the short run. I may have to do some things that are uncomfortable in the short run to help you do what you need to do. But if I love how you make me feel, I love this feeling of infatuation. And when the infatuation slips away, I stop loving you. And we can't let that happen so we become obsessed with keeping the infatuation alive and intense all the time. People can't stay infatuated forever. Infatuation comes and goes. It starts, then grows, and then disappears.

In addictive relationships, we don't love our partner, we love how our partner makes us feel.

No Perfect Relationship

There is no such thing as a perfect relationship. A relationship is the contact between two human beings who choose to be partners and who love each other. When you love how your partner makes you feel, they are your drug and they have one and only one job: To "blow my mind" on demand! To make me feel the way I want to feel, when I want to feel it. Right now, on demand, anytime I want it, anywhere I want it. And as long as you can do it, I love you and care about you. You are the greatest thing that ever entered my life. But when you stop doing it, you are scum. You are worthless and useless, and you had better shape up and do what is necessary to be a lovable human being. There is a big difference between the two frames of reference.

Gay Relationships

All of these principles for relationships apply to both heterosexual and homosexual couples. It doesn't really make any difference. If there's a strong sexual attraction, regardless of your sexual preference, the dynamics and the psychological features work the same.

If you are in a gay relationship, the only difference is that you have the added problem of being involved in a relationship that doesn't have the support of society. You have to deal with the discriminatory issues that go along with being involved in a relationship that many people don't like.

I also want to dispel some myths. A lot of straight people come to me and say that all gay people are into these addictive, promiscuous-type relationships. The fact is, many gay people are in very mature, responsible, long-term, loving, caring relationships. They are not promiscuous, and they don't act out sexually in irresponsible ways. This is important for everyone to realize.

My experience with the gay community shows the same general profile of people as in the straight community. We're all struggling to find love, care, and affection, and to move into healthy, committed relationships. Once we can recognize that the core needs are basically the same, we can move beyond the discrimination and stereotypes that keep us apart instead of bringing us together.

Intensity

Four factors cause intensity in an addictive relationship. Once you understand what creates it, you can learn how to channel it. I use an acronym SAAD to describe the intensity factors of addictive relationships, which are really very sad.

Addictive Relationships Are SAAD

S = Sexuality
A = Anticipation
A = Affirmation
D = Danger

The S stands for *sexuality.* Addictive relationships thrive on a sexual bond between partners. Both partners either feel, or they pretend to feel, strong sexual attraction. Pretend is an important word here. When people have intense reactions to each other, it is common for one partner to be bonded primarily because of strong sexual intensity and for the other partner to value the sexual intensity little or not at all. They're in the relationship for totally different reasons.

Anticipation, which represents the first A in the SAAD equation, is one of the other reasons. We meet somebody and anticipate that they are going to fill us up and make us feel whole and complete. This anticipation, this idea of the one who's going to fix us, really draws and attracts us into the relationship.

The second A is *affirmation.* In the beginning we are with someone who is on their best relationship behavior.

They're affirming us and telling us we're okay, that we're highly desirable as a man or a woman.

Finally, the D is *danger.* Danger creates an adrenaline rush that heightens everything else. It's interesting to note that people in healthy relationships are typically more interested in safety than they are in danger.

Danger

Risk-taking and danger are present in every relationship. To risk being in love is to risk being abandoned. To risk valuing someone is to risk losing the person who you value. But part of the danger element is natural. To be alive is to risk dying, and any time you have something of value, you risk losing it. But there also is such a thing as *pathological risk-taking behaviors.* For example, to have sex on the first date with a stranger without using a condom is a life-threatening experience today because of AIDS and other sexually transmitted diseases. You'd better get to know who your partner is, and you'd better be sure that they're disease-free before you start acting out sexually. While it gives you a big adrenaline kick to get involved sexually with a stranger in an irresponsible way, it's also extremely dangerous behavior.

To see the pathological danger carried to the extreme, rent the movie *Looking for Mr. Goodbar.* You will get in touch with the frenzied type of pathological risk-taking that goes along with many extremely addictive relationships. This type of danger-seeking is not healthy. If you want healthy, productive love, you've got to abstain from that type of behavior. Then you can get into healthy forms of excitement-seeking.

Some partners are primarily motivated for sexuality and danger. Counterdependent styles—the overt controller, the top dogs—fall into this category. Codependent players are typically motivated by anticipation and affirmation. They know their partner can fill them up, make them whole and complete, and save them from themselves. They're willing to tolerate the demands for constant high-intensity sex and for the other dangerous things that they're invited into in order for the partner to get their satisfaction.

But that's not why they're bonded in. The counterdependent player is after sexuality and danger and typically believes their partner wants the same thing. And, of course, the person who's into it for anticipation and affirmation believes their partner wants what they want. So here's what you run into: One partner says, "I am really affirming you, making you feel all right, and telling you you're a good person. So why aren't you happy?" The other person says, "I don't want that stuff. I want sex!" So as the relationship unfolds and both people start presenting their hidden, unspoken agendas to one another, there are massive surprises in store.

I remember the horrible experience of being confronted once by my partner. She said, "I don't enjoy the sexual aspect of the relationship because I don't like the way you treat me sexually." And I had thought she loved it. I thought that it was a mutually satisfying experience, while she was only tolerating it in order to get other aspects from the relationship.

That confrontation marked one of my major moves into personal growth because I had a choice. I could say, "Well, forget her. I'm not going to put up with this. My male ego is shattered. I'm going to leave and go find someone who *likes* having sex with me." But I was intrigued enough to stay. I also realized that there was something here for me to learn. The idea that there was something else in the relationship besides sex was new to me. I had never really contemplated that before. I had talked to clients about it, but it had never dawned on me that it was true in my life, as well.

Therapists go through all kinds of schizophrenia in telling patients how to do things right. I asked a therapist friend once, "What is mental health?" and he looked at me and answered, "Terry, mental health is what we tell our clients to do, but seldom do ourselves."

Codependents who need anticipation and affirmation believe their partner is as needy as they are. And, typically, that's not true. But they don't understand that. One woman I talked to told me she was crushed because her partner left her. She felt she should have seen it coming. When I asked her why, she replied, "On our first date, before we ever got involved, he warned me. "You don't want to get involved with me," he told her over coffee one night. "I am a woman user and I'm scared of intimacy. I don't want to make a commitment and if it gets too heavy, I will leave." And just when the relationship started going somewhere, he left.

"I never believed him. I thought he was just saying that." She thought he was just as needy as she was. But he was into a using type of dynamic rather than a need-to-be-fixed type of dynamic.

Safety

In tying this up, addictive relationships are intensity without substance—sexuality, anticipation, affirmation, and danger with no substance to balance it. No shared values, no shared goals, no shared life-style preferences. And, as a result, it becomes passion minus safety.

> Addictive relationships are passion minus safety!

Healthy relationships are intensity with substance, not boredom with substance. You cannot have high substance with really boring people, people you'd rather not be around. The trick is to find somebody with whom there is some chemistry and intensity. Your preference structures should match well enough so that it's easy to turn yourself on to him or her. You shouldn't have to work at this. Yet you should share values, goals, and life-style preferences. The result is passion *plus* safety.

It's possible to seek safe, fulfilling, passionate, and intense relationships without the element of danger. If the relationship is going to survive in the long run, both partners must feel inherently safe with each other. It's the primary feature.

How-to's of Relationship Building

Relationship building and transforming include some real how-to aspects. How do you communicate with your partner in a healthy way to resolve issues? How do you get into relationships that grow instead of recycle?

First, there's relationship abstinence. If you have a history of really dysfunctional relationships, and you're at a loss for what's causing these relationships to be dysfunctional or what's causing them to blow up in your face, you may need to abstain from relationships for a period of time.

The concept of abstinence has two components. The first is abstaining from dysfunctional behaviors. Even if you're in a committed relationship, you are going to have to stop acting out in immature, punitive, and irresponsible ways. You need to learn to get control of your obsessive thoughts, to learn how not to act on your compulsive feelings, and to learn how to constrain yourself. You need to realize that certain partners are wrong for you, and you need to realign your romantic turn-ons.

One woman told me she couldn't understand her relationship failures. She was a recovering alcoholic who had been sober for three years. She didn't have any relationships for the first year, and over the next two she got involved in three serious relationships. In all three, the partners physically beat her.

I asked her where she went to meet these guys, and she told me she met them in biker bars, because these were the kinds of guys who turned her on. Then she went into a whole song and dance about how bikers have a bad reputation and that they are really warm, caring, generous, nurturing people underneath. It's just that society doesn't understand them. When you see beyond the initial image, they are really worthwhile people.

While this may be true, she would also associate with bikers who were heavy drinkers. By doing this, she was associating with partners who have a high-risk profile for getting into an abusive relationship with her. Women who want a higher-than-average risk of being beaten should pick up a drunk biker.

I asked her if she would consider trying to experiment with different types of partners. She said that no one else turned her on, saying, "Where do you want me to go—to church or something?"

If you are into heavy-duty dysfunctional relationships, you have a dysfunctional partner profile in your mind. You have trained yourself to turn on to that kind of partner, and you don't know how to turn yourself on to any other kind of partner. You perceive other partners as either boring or threatening. So you keep going back to what you are familiar with. You will need to abstain from this.

Abstinence

Relationship abstinence is not the long-term goal. The goal is to get into a relationship so that you can begin to develop relationship skills. Abstaining from relationships gives you a period of time to heal from your previous relationship and to work on yourself. It allows you to learn who you are so you can fill up that emotional hunger within yourself. When you've got your own act together, then you can get involved in a relationship. If you get involved in a relationship before this, it will just confuse your therapy. You've got to get enough of an anchor, enough solidity with yourself to be able to relate to another human being. Otherwise, you instantly lose yourself in your partner. You're gone.

Many people are surprised when they abstain from a relationship for three, four, or five years. They go through therapy, meet their inner child, develop a good relationship with their inner child, heal their past pain, and get to where they're feeling really good as a highly healthy, independently functional person. Then they decide to get into relationships again. They go out, see the same type of person, and the same sparks fire. They get into the exact same relationship as before, and even though they're on good terms with their inner child, they're back into the same old stuff.

This happens because they're refusing to recognize one basic thing: *You can't develop relationship skills by refusing to be in a relationship.* It's like saying, I want to become a good basketball player and because I have all kinds of bad habits, I'll just stop playing basketball for three months. The bad habits don't just go away.

You can't develop relationship skills by refusing to be in a relationship.

Relationship Skills

Relationships involve skills. People hate to hear this. I demystify relationships all the time. If you want to be in an effective relationship, you have to develop skills. You have to know how to do it.

If your parents had done a good job parenting you, they would have taught you, by word and example, the skills of building a relationship. But they probably didn't. As a result, a large percentage of our adult population has never had basic training in relationship skill-building, and they're operating on totally dysfunctional skills.

My approach to relationship building differs from people who focus on the reclaiming yourself. They say once you've reclaimed yourself, you'll automatically be able to have a healthy relationship. My experience doesn't tell me that. When you reclaim yourself, you know how to have a good relationship with you. It doesn't teach you how to have a good relationship with someone else. And when you get involved in relationships again, the old tapes are reactivated, producing a compulsion to act out in the same old ways.

So what we really need is a two-stage relational recovery model. Stage one is learning how to get your act together for you. Remember, first the self, then the possibility of healthy love. There's plenty of good stuff on this. John Bradshaw has some excellent materials on how to reclaim yourself. Once you have started making significant strides in reclaiming yourself, you need a new road map on how to build intimate relationships and what to do. And this is what we're going to deal with.

Healthy Intimacy

The first thing you have to do is make room for healthy intimacy. This means you've got to start some sort of personal recovery program. Twelve Step programs are wonderful—CODA, Al-Anon, ACOA, Sex and Love Addicts are a few. But my observations and experience tell me that when it comes to relationship recovery, Twelve Step programs alone are usually not sufficient. Your rate of recovery will accelerate if you also get into therapy with someone who understands both psychotherapy and strategies for relationship-building skills. If your problem is big enough to warrant going to CODA or ACOA, it's big enough to warrant an investment in good therapy. You will speed up your progress and won't get stuck in your recovery process.

Abstain from Dysfunctional Behavior

The second thing you need to do is to abstain from dysfunctional relationship behaviors. Your first step is to make a list of these behaviors, which usually means breaking your denial.

This denial takes the form of blaming the other person. If I'm in a dysfunctional relationship, it's my partner's problem: "I'm this healthy, well-functioning, recovery-oriented human being who's living with the bloody psychopath who is making my life miserable. And if he or she would only shape up...." Or, "I'm this healthy, functional, together, self-confident person who's living with this wimpy codependent who is unwilling to get into recovery."

This is where you've got to start owning some responsibility. One guy came into therapy, saying that he didn't understand his problem. He was married to a woman who was an idiot. She was dumb and stupid and couldn't figure anything out, and he constantly had to take charge of her. I asked him if this was his first marriage; he said no, it was his fourth. And all of his previous wives were dumber than stones, as well. I asked him if he had dated between his marriages. He answered that he dated while he was married, but all of those women were stupid, too. This guy actually felt that all women were idiots. He wanted me to teach him how to have an intimate relationship with dumb women.

This was a challenge. I wanted to ask him a question but warned him that he wouldn't like the question. So I asked him for a commitment that he wouldn't leave the office and that he would deal with his emotional reaction. He agreed, so I asked, "What is it about you that attracts all these stupid women? In my experience, there are some very intelligent women out there. Apparently none of them want anything to do with you. So I wonder, what is it about you that repels women with an IQ above ten and attracts all the women who just don't think, who turn off their brains?"

What is it about some women that attracts abusive men? What is it about them that pushes or scares away nice guys? Why do some men repel intelligent women? What is it about some men that attracts screwed up women?

There's a term in recovery called becoming proactive. This means you take responsibility for your part. It's not all your fault, but you have to own your responsibility. You have to realize that there is an interaction between my issues, your issues, and our issues. "If I don't have a problem, I'm not going to tolerate yours. If I am tolerating your problem, and it's interfering with my ability to be happy, that's my problem." And you've got to ask what is it about me that says I'm defenseless against this? What is it about me that prevents me from putting up a boundary, setting a limit, making a demand, or getting out? What's my part in all this?

> Being proactive in relationship means that you take responsibility for your part of the problems.

The relationship behaviors that have to be abstained from are behaviors of commission and omission. In my case, I'm a recovering counterdependent, one of those top dog, take charge, "turn people into objects and use them" kind of guy. That's my background. I had to abstain from controlling, manipulating, and objectifying my partner. And I had to start doing things like listening, noticing what my partner feels, and caring about what my partner thinks. I had to learn how to become sensitive. The rewards have been there but in the beginning, it was awful. I had to realize there's a world populated with other people.

Codependents have to learn to abstain from being passive, from passively accepting everything that happens to them as God's will. They have to learn how to set up boundaries and limits, to make demands or to get out. And it may require therapy to do this. Here's an example of a dialogue that is *not* codependent.

Codependent: "Excuse me, I'm not going to let you do that to me anymore. You need to stop doing that!" *I'm being very clear, very concrete, no double message, here at all.* "It is not acceptable for you to yell at me and to use profanity. That stops right now. And if you are not willing to stop it, then I'll have to consider what further steps I need to take to not be subjected to that because it hurts me, it humiliates me, it degrades me, and I'm not willing to accept that from you. And if you're not going to stop the behavior, then I have to decide what I'm going to do so that you can behave how you want, but so that I don't get victimized by it."

Partner: "You're trying to control me. What right do you have to control me?"

Codependent: "I'm not trying to control you. I'm telling you that your behavior is unacceptable and that you have to make a choice. If using profanity toward me is more important than staying in a relationship with me, that's the choice I'm asking you to make. That's not a control, it's asking you to make a choice. And if you choose your need to use profanity over the relationship with me, I need that information to consider what I'm going to do about it."

Once you have abstained from dysfunctional partners and relationship behaviors, and you have learned some basic control over your own thinking, feelings and behaviors, the next step is to build a foundation for a relationship.

High-risk Profiles

Let's examine how to build a relationship. All of us have already established in our minds the concept of a person whom I will call a high-risk partner profile. We need to identify the characteristics of these people and recognize them as high risks. It's similar to the way they check for terrorists at airports. Anyone wearing army fatigues and carrying a can of gasoline or a plastic explosive needs to be checked out.

To find your own high-risk partner profile, take every destructive relationship you've ever been in, list their names, and individually describe the *physical characteristics* of each person—tall, short, dark, light, fat, thin, muscular, and so on. Put down any physical things that attracted you to each person. Now write down their *personality traits,* their psychological characteristics—shy, gregarious, active, passive, kind, mean. Next, note their *social characteristics*—lots of friends, no friends, deep friendships, superficial friendships, wanted to be with people, wanted to be alone. And finally, describe *what each person hooked in you* and allowed you to be turned on. What was the fantasy or attraction? What could they do for you that you could not do for yourself? Do the same for every past relationship you've had. Then you do it for your mother and father. And if you weren't raised with your natural mother or father, do it for your primary caretakers. You'll see a pattern emerge.

When we see a person who matches our high-risk physical profile (in other words their looks "turn me on"), we instantly assume that this person meets the psychological and social aspects of the profile as well. Their appearance causes us to assume that we know this person in-depth when we don't.

In addition to the physical characteristics, there's a psychological high-risk personality profile. Ever wonder what the attraction is between physically mismatched people? The only answer I had to this until recently was my grandmother's saying that "God makes them and God matches them." For some people the physical is very important and with others, it's not important. Some get hooked by the psychological features. So you have to list the personality characteristics, too. If you're with a high-risk personality profile person, you feel bonded with them instantly. You're soul mates. And if you believe in karma, you know you've shared past lives together.

There's also a social aspect of it, the matching of life-style preferences. You have to take the mirror image and say, "Of these things, what is getting hooked in me." Then you're prepared to make a decision when you meet somebody, whether this is a high-risk person or not.

Sometimes we get disillusioned quickly. I've got my high-risk partner profile, and this doesn't mean I don't get involved with them, it means that I go on guard. A red warning signal goes beep, beep, beep. Go conscious now, do not go unconscious. If you go unconscious, you can be in big trouble. Stay awake, stay alert, this may be a friend or it may be a foe. You don't know. You're going to have to take extra precautions.

Years ago, I saw my classic high-risk partner across the room, and I knew I was in love. I "knew" she was a ballet dancer interested in martial arts and that she was a highly spiritual person, very intelligent, probably aspiring to a master's or doctoral degree in psychology. So I walked up to her and introduced myself. She turned around and couldn't speak English. Maybe all those things were true, but we could not even communicate with each other. Now that taught me something.

The next step in building a healthy relationship is laying the foundation. This starts with the three C's of intimacy: Communication, Caring, and Commitment.

The Three C's of Intimacy:

1. Communication
2. Caring
3. Commitment

Communication

When you see a high-risk person or anyone attractive, you proceed to communicate with them. Communication is an exchange of ideas, thoughts, and feelings. You start by talking first. As you communicate with somebody, you share something about yourself and see how the person responds. If you get a negative response, you stop. This is a strange notion for some.

Healthy sharing starts off with low-level risks. You share something like your name. "Hi, I'm Terry." If you get a response like, "Yea? So what," you think, gee, I don't want to talk to this person, and you move on.

If I'm very codependent, I say to myself, she's just scared and unable to make contact with me, and she needs me to reach out to her. I can change her. I will try harder. My parents were alcoholics, and I used to be very shy, too, and I know how she feels. Now you're off and running on your way to a very destructive relationship.

Healthy people have this continuum of sharing. They start out very safely saying, "This is who I am, and this is what I'm about. Here's my public self." And then if the person responds in a way that is satisfactory to them, they then take a risk and go a step deeper. But if the person doesn't respond in a way that says that this person is safe to communicate with, they stop at that level or they disconnect all together.

To a potentially healthy partner, you say something like, "Hi, I'm Terry Gorski, and I just want to meet you." She says, "My name is whatever, and I'm glad you walked over because I saw you, too, and I thought you looked like an interesting person. I'd like to meet you."

I took a little risk, shared it with her, and she went a little deeper and invited me to another level. So now I can say, "Well, I noticed you, too, and you look like an interesting person. What do you do?"

Now there is mutual risk-taking going on. Beware of relationships where there is no mutuality, no mutual risk-taking. You can tell this if you go home from a date and you know absolutely nothing about your partner—and he or she knows everything about you.

One of my patients said she had been dating a guy for seven months and just found out he was married. How is this possible? You have to go unconscious. I asked if he ever gave her his home phone number. Did he tell you where he worked? Did you ever go out on holidays? "No" answers to questions like these reveal a pattern. What did you do last Christmas? "He said he had to be out of town," she replied. Then I asked the key question. "Did you ever ask him about these things?" She said "No!" Where was the communication?

A number of years ago, a big Mafia leader was indicted, and I saw his wife on one of the talk shows. She was now writing a big exposé book to tide her over until her husband could get out. The host asked her how she could be married for more than eighteen years to a man who was a Mafia leader. She looked at him in all seriousness and said, "I never knew what he did for a living." Eighteen years of marriage and she may not have been lying. She may have gone unconscious. That's why communication is important.

Communication must come first. Once you communicate with someone, you start to know about the other person by exchanging information. You can only care about somebody that you know. It's another fundamental principle. You can have a general love for all of humankind but you don't sleep with all of humankind on a first date.

Caring

Communication allows you to decide whether you care enough about the person to move to the next relationship level. Caring means you are concerned enough to value this person. Now here's where we get into trouble, especially for codependents. We believe caring is all or nothing, black or white. We either care or we don't. Suppose I'm married and I care about my wife. Suppose we have a housekeeper who I care about, also. Now if they are both in life-threatening situations, and I can only attend to one, I'll go to my wife first. I care about her more than my housekeeper. This is called values clarification. We need to have the capacity to say how much we care and how much time, energy, and resources we are willing to commit to this person.

I will lend a small amount of money to my housekeeper, but I won't burden myself with loans to pay for her medical treatment. But if my wife is sick, I would hock everything I owned to pay for her care. There's a difference in caring levels. Many people don't know that you can choose how much you care based on the knowledge of who your partner is; what their values, goals, and life-style preferences are; compatibility; and how well that person meets your needs. I only make high-level commitments to people who are essential to my well-being, people who I care a lot about, and who I want in my supportive circle.

Healthy Social Networks

There's an exercise to demonstrate a healthy social network. I put a dot in the middle of the room and suggest you stand on the dot. Then I tell the group that it is their job to get as physically close to you as possible. Everyone comes up and tries to press in as close as they can, but with thirty people in the group, only four or five people can fit around you physically. Now one person is going to be right in front, another off the side where you can easily relate to him or her, and two people will be in the back where they are close but you have a hard time relating to them. This becomes your primary intimate circle.

The person who faces you straight off should ideally be your primary love partner. Then you physically have room for two very close friends, maybe three. The people behind you, those guarding your back, are typically work associates who you rely on not to fire you, to get you a paycheck, to support you. This completes your close, intimate network: your lover, your friends, your colleagues or mentors.

Then there's the second circle of people who you can reach out and touch, who are there when you want them. These are companions and people with whom you share activities and go to parties. Finally, there's another circle out there, and you can't even touch these people. You know they're there, and you can wave.

Like it or not, this is reality. You don't just randomly let anyone push their way into your inner circle. If you leave it to random chance, you'll get someone who you don't like trying to be close to you. You must be proactive and choose, saying, "Excuse me, would you get out of the way to let this one in here." It takes a great level of self-confidence and self-worth to be able to do this.

If you want to build your life and have the kind of relationship that works for you, you've got to decide how much you care about each person and then negotiate how you want people involved in your life. We've all had situations where we want to be right up front, in someone's inner circle, and he or she has pushed us away, saying, "No, thank you. I really like you, but not here. I want you either over here or a circle back." And it hurts when this happens, but that's life. There will be times when people want to put themselves in your face and you've got to turn them away. It may hurt them, but life hurts.

To have a life that works means that we sometimes inflict pain on other people. But don't overestimate your power to hurt others. I'm responsible for my pain and how I deal with it; you are responsible for your pain and how you deal with it. I am not responsible for your pain. If I live in fear of asserting myself—attending to my needs and my wants—for fear of hurting other people, I become immobilized and will end up hurting you worse.

Commitment

Once you decide at what level you care, then you can decide at what level you're going to commit. In healthy relationships, you communicate first, thoroughly getting to know who your partner is and what their life is about. Then you decide the level of caring. You communicate with each other and make a decision to care at one level, which leads to an appropriate commitment. Then you communicate some more. If, out of that communication, you find out this person has more value still, you care about them at a higher level and negotiate a higher order of commitment.

Communication cannot occur as a one-way street. Many people believe that because I have self-disclosed to my partner, we have communicated. Communication doesn't occur until your partner reciprocates and self-discloses to you at the same level. To tell your partner everything you think and feel, and to have him or her tell you nothing, is *not* communicating. That's having a monologue.

People in dysfunctional relationships see someone across the room, know it's the one and only, and make a high-level commitment: "This is it. That's her, the one and only for all of eternity. She's going to have my babies, and we're going to live together happily ever after. I will do anything to make this thing work." You care about her so much you obsess about her and build a massive fantasy of who she is. You whomp up all of this high-level caring and then walk up and say hello. But before you begin to communicate, before she even responds, you're already committed to the relationship. To solve this problem, you have to reverse the process, and this is hard to do.

If you're going to have an effective love relationship, you need to develop platonic love. Platonic love means friendship. It's the kind of love you feel with a nonsexual friend. You need to build the platonic dimensions and to act on the different levels of relationship with your lover. But you also have a whole new dimension to build which is erotic love. This is the type of experience we develop with someone to whom we are sexually attracted, regardless of the nature of the sexual preference.

Relationship Building and Relationship Transforming

Before you stand a chance of having a healthy relationship, you have to stop acting out in overtly dysfunctional ways with your current partner. And if you have a partner who is unwilling or unable to build a relationship with you, you have to disconnect from him or her and find a willing partner.

It continually amazes me that so many people have the illusion that they are in a relationship when they're not. One woman came to me at a workshop, saying that she has been married to a man for nine years. "He has had over fourteen affairs, and he's not even subtle about it. I've asked him to stop, and he won't. What should I do?"

"Leave him," I said. "He's not in a relationship with you anymore." But she said she couldn't leave because they had a commitment. And I said no, they didn't have a commitment, *she* had a commitment. He had nothing to do with it.

A commitment in a relationship is an agreement or a contract. It is only valid as long as both partners honor it. When your partner violates the contract, the contract is null and void. You then have full right, if you choose to exercise it, in clear conscience, to renegotiate it.

People don't understand that the relationship contract gets renegotiated many times in the course of the relationship. You don't stay in the same relationship for twenty years. You stay in a relationship with the same person, but the people who succeed at long-term relationships renegotiate. And each period of renegotiation is scary because a renegotiation basically means that one partner is not willing to hold up his or her end of the agreement anymore. He or she is not willing to be in the old relationship and wants to change the agreement. When you negotiate a change in a relationship, there's always the possibility that the relationship may end. And there is a double-edge sword here. If you don't renegotiate to get your new emerging needs met, the relationship will end anyway. We either do the negotiations up front, honestly and consciously, or we go underground and destroy the relationship unconsciously.

I remember being single and scared to death of intimacy. I couldn't find a quality woman, and I didn't understand why. I was dating about six women at the same time, sleeping with them all, unknown to each other, and couldn't understand why a high-quality woman wouldn't appear in my life. None of the women I was dating, in my mind, had the potential for a long-term, lasting relationship. And I was dating these women to kill time until the right one came along.

So I went to a therapist to work on what I could do to attract the right woman. He talked to me about the image I was conveying. If a high-quality woman did come around, why would she want to get involved with a guy who was dating six women at once?

I can't emphasize enough that if you want to have a bunch of short-term, noncommitted sexual relationships, enjoy them. But realize that if you are looking for a quality partner in a committed relationship, you will probably have to end your freewheeling life-style *before* the high-potential partner appears. If you should meet a high-quality person, and she finds out about the kind of life-style you are living, she'll probably look for someone with a different type of life-style.

There's an inherent leap of faith in relationship building where you have to envision where you are going. You have to begin with your end in mind and then make changes.

Most people believe relationships are things that happen to us over which we have little or no control. That's because we don't understand the process of relating. Most people say they want a relationship. But a relationship is not a thing, it is a process. It changes your whole mind-set to say, "I want to be *in the process of relating* to another human being." Then, of course, it raises the question of how you want to relate and how you want your partner to relate to you. This process brings us into the realm of why relationships are so difficult.

I have periods in my current relationship when I relate as a fully responsible, high-integrity, loving, caring partner, and then I have days when I abdicate and back away from the process. There are days when my partner is able to respond to me in a wide-open, honest, healthy relationship process kind of way, and there are other days when she isn't.

You don't find a healthy relationship, you find a partner who's willing to engage in a relationship process, and then you strive to have an honest, open, mutually beneficial process going on between the two of you. And then you've got to realize that we're fallible human beings, and we all have bad days.

Acquaintanceship

Once you find a partner who's willing to do it, here's how you start. There are platonic aspects of a relationship and erotic or sexual aspects of a relationship. This division is very important and gets very complicated if you don't honor it.

The Levels of Platonic Relationships

1. Acquaintanceship
2. Companionship
3. Friendship
4. Partnership

The first level of a platonic relationship is *acquaintanceship.* When you're going out to build a relationship with anyone, you need to have acquaintances from which to choose. This comes as big news to most people from dysfunctional families. They believe that while they're living in splendid isolation, all of a sudden, the god or goddess of their choice will appear in front of them. And they have no idea how this happens. They expect them to pop up suddenly in the supermarket or magically while they're walking on the street.

Healthy people realize that there's no magic involved. If you're looking for a potential partner, you're going to have to meet forty to fifty people before you find one with whom you feel comfortable. The laws of chance will dictate that with this many, you will meet someone who has sufficient compatibilities and substance with you, and to whom you will be willing to commit and care about. So this means that you have to have some kind of vehicle in your life to meet people.

Single people often make the mistake of cruising, going out looking for romantic partners. It doesn't work that way. I took questions at a workshop once and someone asked, "Terry, after the first half of your workshop, I got so depressed that I couldn't cruise the audience during the break. How long will this last?"

The trick to finding a partner is this: *Get a Life!* A partner is designed to share your life with you. If you get out of a relationship and put your life on hold, that's the problem. You need to get interests. Find things that you like to do. And to get a life means you develop warm, cordial relationships with a large number of acquaintances.

Acquaintances are people with whom you are polite and friendly, but to whom you have no commitments. This includes waitresses, waiters, coworkers with whom you don't work very closely, people you meet on the street, neighbors down the hall in your apartment building, and people you see at large, open Twelve Step meetings who you don't know very well. The larger your acquaintanceship network, the more likely it is that you'll be able to connect with somebody who has the potential to be a good, healthy, loving, caring partner. There is no mystery or magic to the process. It's not past karma, it's simply probability. If you want to increase the likelihood of connecting with a potential partner who matches with you, you have to meet more people. You also have to have a notion in mind of what you want. And it's helpful to have realistic expectations.

I find that people have two problems when it comes to expectations in partners. Most people have expectations that are down in the gutter somewhere. If they breathe and their heart beats, they're acceptable. "I can't have high standards, because what decent person would go out with me?" This low self-esteem works against you even with acquaintances. You think there must be something wrong with anyone who wants to know you. So the minute someone shows an interest, you believe they must be flawed. It's the old Groucho Marx syndrome: "I'd never join a club that would allow someone like me to be a member."

When people build acquaintanceship networks, you must build them without the primary goal of finding a lover. A lot of people don't understand this. I told one of my patients that he'd probably meet an acceptable partner within twelve to eighteen months if he did as I suggested. He was a police officer whose life consisted mainly of working, going to AA meetings, and going to bed (usually alone). I told him that he had to get a life, to find some interests outside of work.

After much prodding, he told me that he was fascinated with guns, so I suggested he join a gun club. The first step in building a social network is to find something you like, and it doesn't matter if anyone else likes it because if you like it, you will meet others who like it, too. You can start in the yellow pages under clubs, whether its hiking, skiing, archaeology, or guns.

So this guy joined a gun club and came back very angry. He went to the first meeting, and there were no women there. I told him he was missing the point. He wasn't going there to meet a lover. I sent him back to find the guys he liked and to begin building a friendship with them.

He came back with two friends. I asked if they were married, and they were. Now if he likes guns and belongs to a gun club, and these two guys like guns and belong to a gun club, they're probably married to women who like guys who like guns. So I told him to have a dinner party and to invite the new friends and their wives over. He objected, saying he wasn't going to cut in on a guy's wife.

He wasn't getting this yet. I explained that these women will check him out to see if he has any bodies in the basement, or any open, running sores, or if he's a nice, personable type of person. And the one thing most women have is girlfriends who, chances are, also like guys who like guns.

So now, I told him, he's likely to get an invitation to a party or a dinner in the near future, and guess who's going to be there: a single, available woman, one of the massive hordes of single, available women who can't find an acceptable partner out there, and she is being subtly fixed up with him. He may not hit it off with the first one, or the second or third. But if he's got his social network going, available women will start appearing. Eventually, he hit it off with one well enough to take the acquaintanceship level into the next level, which is companionship.

It works the same with women. You need to develop a broad network of women friends, and then invite the men with whom they are involved into your life in a social way. Almost every guy who has an adequate social life knows other guys who are available and who want to meet nice women. If your friend has any integrity, he's not going to fix you up with a loser because he's going to see you again. Besides that, his girlfriend or wife is your friend and he will consider that when making the introduction.

When building acquaintanceship networks, it's important to build them without the primary goal of finding a lover. You are there to have a good time, to enjoy yourself, to do something that interests you. This takes the pressure off and allows you to be yourself. Then, through your network, people will surface. Rarely have I met people who have succeeded at finding a romantic interest when their goal was to do that. Normally, a potential partner surfaces out of the natural fabric of the person's social network.

Being a recovering alcoholic, I prowled bars for years looking for a relationship. I never found a relationship in a bar that lasted more than three dates. Yet I have had four serious love relationships in my life, and in each of them, the person just appeared out of my social network. It's the social network that allows that to happen.

You need to get on an acquaintanceship level with a variety of members of the same and opposite sex. And you don't have to be sexually attracted to them. In fact, it is helpful if you are not.

Companionship

Once you've established an acquaintanceship, you can then invite the person into the next level which is *companionship.* In an acquaintanceship, you meet someone superficially but you have no commitments to them at all. When you move to companionship, you invite this person to share a preferred activity with you. But the activity is more important than the person.

You are a person who enjoys playing tennis. You see somebody in your acquaintanceship network who you'd like to get to know better. Instead of planning an intimate, romantic, candle-lit dinner in your apartment, you invite this person to play tennis. Tell him or her that you are putting together a game of doubles tennis for Saturday, and ask if they would like to join you at the tennis club at two o'clock. If the person says no, perhaps because they don't like tennis, you say, "Too bad, I guess I'll have to find someone else to make up the foursome." Here, the activity is more important than the person.

If you have a history of destructive relationships, and if you have a hard time asserting your needs and wants, it's very important for you to learn how to conduct a companionship. A companionship means there's something that you want to do that's not negotiable, but you want to share the activity so you invite someone to share it with you. And if they say no, you find someone else to do it.

You need companionship skills even when you're in a committed relationship to keep your individuality. Suppose I like action, science-fiction, Terminator-type movies and my wife doesn't. I don't deprive myself of an enjoyable activity just because she doesn't like them as much as I do. I go with a friend who likes these types of movies.

When I go to a science-fiction movie with another friend instead of my wife, we are operating on a companionship level because I'm treating her like a companion. And she understands that so she's not offended. In this instance, I didn't say, "I want to spend an evening with you." I said, "I want to go to this movie and would you care to join me?"

Maybe there are things that she likes to do that I don't—for example, going to art fairs. She likes to go and I don't. So when there's an art fair, she's free to go with another friend. Now we had major wars over this kind of stuff early in our relationship. When I invited her to see a movie with me, she thought I wanted to spend private time with her when I really wanted to see the movie. She was crushed. And when I refused to go to an art fair with her after the third or fourth miserable time, she thought I was abandoning her.

Both of you need to understand the companionship level. Then you can shatter the relationship myth that both partners share all the same interests. No two people share all the same interests. *If two people agree about everything, one of them is unnecessary.* And simply, if you have a partner who enjoys something that you don't like, you don't have to do it with him or her. But it means you're going to have to negotiate on the companionship level. You need to say, "When I do this, you don't like it. I don't want to see you miserable. It kills my good time. And when we do that, I don't like it. It makes me miserable. So let's agree that you can do this by yourself and I can do that by myself, and we can do these other things together."

Problems in negotiating companionships arise when you find out that you have very little in common. Incompatibility is the term for this. Now many incompatible people negotiate and compromise their entire life and make their relationship grow, but generally, they have to work very hard at it. They have to invest high levels of energy, and they are usually not very happy. The more you have in common, the more shared interests you have, the better the relationship is going to be and the easier it is going to be to maintain it.

Once you've got your companionship going, you see the person in a different arena. If you're dating, the best companionships include group activities. You want to see how your partner is going to interact with groups, and you want him to meet your friends. The exact opposite is usually true in addictive relationships. Here, you meet somebody, and you just disappear from your friendship circles for a period of time. You go into romantic isolation with your partner. None of your friends get to meet your partner, so they can't give you any feedback, and you don't really want any. You want to enjoy the infatuation undisturbed until it blows up.

Friendship

The next level invites the person into a *friendship.* You still share activities with friends but the focus is different. In a friendship, the focus of the activity is to spend time with that specific person.

These levels work with platonic as well as erotic relationships. I have a very close male friend, and there are a lot of activities that we enjoy together. But sometimes, he calls me up to say he wants to do this, and I say that I don't feel like doing that tonight. Then he says, "That's okay, because I really want to just spend time with you and to catch up." Then we figure out something else to do because the primary purpose is to spend time together.

There's a willingness to negotiate the activity because the activity is simply a vehicle or an excuse to be together. "Let's have dinner together," isn't that I want to go to this restaurant and eat this food. It's that I want an excuse to sit down and spend time with a friend.

If you invite someone into a friendship when they're not a companion first, your warning signals should go off. If you haven't been in a companionship relationship, you don't know enough to commit to a level of a friendship. As you move from acquaintanceship to companionship, you're now making activity-oriented commitments. You're investing time, energy, and resources, and you're making promises to which your partner has the right to hold you accountable. When you move up into a friendship, there are even more serious commitments.

Partnership

The final level of this continuum is to move into *partnership.* A partnership occurs when two people share legally or morally binding agreements with each other. As soon as two people become roommates, there is a legal contract. As soon as you commit money to take an expensive vacation six months from now, you're partners. As soon as you go into business together, you're partners. When someone asks to borrow a thousand dollars, that's a loan and you should have loan papers unless you're legally married.

Most people don't think about the practicality of most relationships. Moving from friendship to partnership is a very serious move. At this point, there are usually legally binding contracts, which means if your partner doesn't like the way you want to work it out, you go to court and the judge decides. Marriage is always a legally binding partnership, as is having a child, whether you are married or not. Even if you don't like each other and you have a child, you are obligated to provide support throughout the child's developmental years.

The Relationship Model

Here's the model of how to move toward partnership. You start with your social network by developing acquaintanceships among this group. Then you invite those you like best into a companionship. You begin sharing activities that you like to do. This allows you to find someone who has common interests, values, and goals. Once you see all this good stuff, you invite one or two into a friendship. You really get to know who they are, to share who you are and to see if a level of in-depth communication can develop. Then if that works out and you really like the person, you move into partnership where you say, "Let's make some commitments to build and share a life together, maybe to conserve costs by combining our apartments. Let's make a partnership, invest in the future, and move ahead in life."

My best friend is a terrific guy, but I would never be his business partner. We have incompatible styles of doing business. It's just that simple. It's not that mine is right and his is wrong, or vice versa, but we have different values, goals, and ways of doing business.

Knowing this model, you can now consciously approach a relationship and ask yourself, "If I'm in a partnership with somebody right now, how is it working out? Do we need to renegotiate? If I'm in a friendship, how is the friendship level working out? How's the companionship? How's the acquaintanceship?"

Shifting Gears

People make another mistake in believing simply because they are in partnership, they can abandon all the friendship activities; because they are friends, they can stop all the companionship activities; because they are companions, they can stop all the acquaintanceship activities. Healthy relationships shift gears constantly. When I get up on a travel day, I've got to get myself together and get to the airport. I am not available for high-level intimacy with my partner, because my mind is on getting to work. I immediately click into an acquaintanceship level, saying, "Hi, how are you," and here's a peck on the cheek. "I've got to get to the airport so get out of my way." We've developed superficial, nice rituals to get us through these high-stress times.

At other times we operate as companions. We go out to movies, shows, parties, and things like that. At times we operate as friends where we spend quiet time together, talking, sharing activities, reviewing the day, taking interest in each other. And then we act as partners, taking care of the household, getting the garbage out, dealing with what we're going to do with our money or lack of it.

We often have conflicts when she invites me into a companionship, and I want to be on a friendship level, and the two don't mesh. But knowing this, we can talk about what the expectations are and understand where the other person is coming from. This is not easy stuff, even if you do it strictly with platonic friends. Building friendships is difficult; it gets even harder when you add an erotic focus.

It is possible to have a purely platonic relationship, even with members of the opposite sex, and never have erotic elements come into it, contrary to *Harry and Sally.*

Some individuals are incapable of it, but it is possible. It is also possible to have an erotic relationship with very little platonic influence to it, a pure sex relationship. And it is also possible to merge the two. Long-lasting love relationships are a combination of the platonic and the erotic, and you can't separate the two.

Many people believe you should develop a nonsexual acquaintanceship that leads to a nonsexual companionship that leads to a nonsexual friendship that leads to a nonsexual partnership where you become nonsexual roommates. Then you feel attracted to each other. That's really nice in theory, and it sometimes happens that way. But it's the exception rather than the rule. Usually there is a building of both platonic and erotic love simultaneously as a relationship grows and develops.

Erotic Level

Let's examine the erotic level and talk about a brazenly pure sexual encounter. You're out to have an erotic relationship, and you're not interested in whether it lasts or it doesn't. You will move the erotic relationship through four levels: attraction, flirtation, sensual involvement, and sexual involvement. Let's look at each of these levels.

The Levels of Erotic Relationship

1. Attraction
2. Flirtation
3. Sensual Involvement
4. Sexual Involvement

Attraction

Erotic relationships begin with attraction. You see someone and you feel attracted to them. If you come from a dysfunctional family, it's probably because your partner meets your high-risk profile. We've been conditioned to feel attracted to what I call "real men" or "real women." This notion is programmed into our unconscious mind when we are little kids. We get the imprint of both mother and father. The mother imprint becomes real woman, and that's what I need to be like if I'm going to be a real woman; if I'm a man, this is what I need to be like. That's the image or imprint that's going to elicit a spontaneous feeling of sexual arousal.

People often deny this but, when you compare the characteristics of past partners to parents, most people find an undeniable and often upsetting similarity. Like it or not, most of us are attracted to partners who combine the characteristics of one or both parents. People who don't physically look, psychologically react, or socially organize like our parents are simply a turn-off. You turn yourself off to these people.

If you find that you are turned on to a particular type of person who has always treated you badly, you need to realign your sexual preferences through individual therapy. You have to learn to turn yourself off to the previous high-risk people and to turn yourself on to healthier, different people. You do this through conscious awareness. Your mind controls your body. Most people think their sex organs are between their legs when they are actually between their ears. And until we start recognizing that sexuality occurs primarily in the mind, we are going to be victimized by the action of our hormones. Sexual arousal is not something that happens automatically when we are stimulated. This is true in animals, not in human beings. Sexual arousal is mediated through the mind.

Most of us are not consciously aware of what we do to turn ourselves on and off. Here's an exercise: When you're with someone who really turns you on (of course, in reality, you turn yourself on to him or her constantly), every fifteen minutes, check out how aroused you are, how turned-on you are to being with him. Almost everybody finds that it varies radically. There are moments when you are really attracted and moments when you are really turned-off. But you rapidly forget the turn-off periods and focus on the period of attraction. Then you romanticize it in your mind by exaggerating it. It's called euphoric recall.

Next, spend some time with someone who turns you off, who you turn yourself off to when you are around him or her. Don't pick a real obnoxious person. Pick someone who is a nice person, but with whom there is no sexual chemistry. Then do the same test, but heighten your awareness. Look at him or her carefully, notice how his body looks and get in touch with your feelings. You will find out there are moments when you feel at least a little sexual arousal.

Now do this exercise with someone of the same sex. Most people find that there is a small capacity to be aroused by people of the same sex. This freaks people out. But we just forget about it completely, and it's gone. We block it out, we repress it.

To change attraction patterns, we have to get into the dynamics of how we turn ourselves on and how we turn ourselves off. Changing attraction patterns is a fundamental prerequisite to getting into a functional relationship. It doesn't do any good to know how to have a healthy relationship if you are only attracted to dysfunctional people. If you had a really destructive high-risk profile programmed into you as a kid, and you are not aware of it, the only one who will turn you on is one who cannot or will not meet your needs. Unless you are willing to take responsibility for changing your preference structure and your arousal or attraction pattern, and for learning to turn yourself on to different types of people, you will be trapped. And, of course, you're going to say, "All that I need is a biker who's sensitive; a prostitute who's loyal; a cat that doesn't crawl on furniture; a fish that doesn't need water."

When you get attracted to someone, it's real strange stuff. Most people are scared to death of sexual attraction, so they control it quite a bit. When people start getting in touch with their sexual attraction, they find out that they can get attracted to a very broad spectrum of different people. And this is frightening because now you have choices. And it's much easier to deaden yourself and not notice your patterns of sexual arousal or attraction.

Noticing

The first step in getting in touch with your patterns of sexual arousal is to notice but not act. I teach people to be able to put on the brakes, to put filters between different levels of sexual response.

The first filter you have is to turn yourself off totally. If you've got a high-risk partner, and you know it's going to be a destructive thing and you don't want to take the risk, you better have the capacity to shut yourself down and turn yourself off. And you *can* control yourself. If you can't, you should be locked away somewhere. Controlling ourselves is the standard of maturity. Learning how is an important aspect of growing up. If you are an adult and never learned how to control yourself, you need to make an appointment with a good therapist and start learning how to do it.

Acknowledging But Not Acting

The next level is to allow yourself to be attracted but not act on it—to feel the attraction and to do nothing with it. You can say to yourself, "Hey, this is kind of neat, but I'm not going to do anything with it. I'm not going to, verbally or nonverbally, let the person I'm attracted to know about it. It will be my private knowing." Now you have a tremendous amount of freedom. If you are able to put this filter up, you can scan a large group of people and feel attracted to three people at the same time. And you can enjoy it. Without communicating it or acting on it, you can be a sexual human being with no risk and no consequences. It gives you some power because all of a sudden, your potential options have expanded. And the attraction doesn't have to go anywhere. This is the mistaken notion that most people make when they get involved in an intimate relationship. It's all or nothing. If I'm attracted, I must go on it. If I feel attracted, I must act on it, move with it. You can feel attracted and do nothing but privately enjoy the attraction.

Healthy people get sexually attracted to many people every day and do absolutely nothing with it by choice. You just stop right there, before it gets out of hand because you have the power to turn yourself off. But you can also choose to move to the next level which is flirtation.

Flirtation

Flirtation is the process of nonverbally and sometimes verbally communicating to somebody that you're sexually interested. People flirt all the time, but most will absolutely deny doing it. A good way to bring it into consciousness is to ask the person, "Are you flirting with me?" And see what happens. All of a sudden it brings a conscious charge into the relationship because now you own your sexual intent. And it doesn't mean you have to do anything about it.

Mature people can acknowledge what they're doing without shame and guilt. If I'm flirting with someone and she asks me if I am, I admit it. And then I return the favor and say, "Are you flirting back?" Now we're on a whole different level of conscious acceptance of what's going on. We can own responsibility for what we're doing with each other and make some conscious choices. The relationship is taken out of the realm of covert manipulation and brought into the realm of honest communication. The problem with most movements in the early stages of flirtation is they are unspoken and often unconscious; the next thing you know, people are in bed with one another. It amazes me how many people go through all these steps of attraction and seduction without ever talking about it.

Having sex with somebody is one of the most complex interpersonal negotiations you're ever going to find. And it is often done without the benefit of language. Think about that level of skill. But when you do it without talking about it, you can feel victimized. You can blame yourself, you can blame your partner, you can feel ashamed. You can say, "I shouldn't have done that. I just lost control of myself." But when you consciously own your flirtations, you make conscious decisions every step of the way. If you are going to flirt, do it, but take responsibility for it.

Moving to Sensuality

At the third level is sensuality. The line between flirtation and sensuality is often a very fine line. There's a big difference in the way you give somebody a hug, in the placement of the arms, the length of the hug, and so on. Walking arm and arm can be done with different intentions. This journey from flirtation to sensuality starts subtly and follows a mating ritual.

You meet someone to whom you're attracted and begin with nonverbal communications, like making eye contact. When the physical contact begins, you shake their hand, but you hold it a little longer. And when you break contact, it's not a clean break. You rub your fingers against the person's palm. Then as you're talking to the person, you make excuses to touch them by accident. As you're walking, you bump into them, and you see if the person bumps back. If they bump back, it's a go signal. Now you bump a little harder and a little longer. You're talking to somebody, and you just reach out and touch their arm. If the person doesn't pull back that's a go signal. So you touch them for a little longer. Then you go from the forearm to the elbow. Now the forearm is a safe zone, but when you move down to the hand, it's an obvious sensual signal.

Most women don't recognize what is going on, or they recognize it and don't trust their own gut-level reaction to flirtation. They either go passive out of fear and disbelief or they give positive responses so as not to hurt the guy's feelings. Women who know the first signals of a flirt will never get hit on by accident. When someone starts flirting, by leaning into her or touching her, she moves away. If he continues, it's hard to be subtle—and she shouldn't be. If she gives no-go messages and he continues, she should turn it verbal and say, "Excuse me, I don't like the way you're touching me. Please stop." It's extremely important for men and women—especially women—to understand this signaling system.

Many women don't know how to set limits at the various and different levels of seduction. A woman who was in therapy with me came in very upset one day. She told me that she had a horrible experience with a co-worker she has known for twelve years. His wife knows her husband. Their children play together. "We've been friends, we've talked, we've shared personal experiences," she said. "Then we went away to a conference together and all of a sudden, for no reason at all, he started kissing me."

How does it happen that all of a sudden, someone is kissing someone? So I asked her to tell me the story.

"Well, it all started when we were both scheduled to go to a sales conference together. He came up to my desk and said, 'I noticed that you're scheduled for the same conference. We've never traveled together. This is exciting.'"

And I said, "Yes, it's exciting."

He then said, "It'll be a good opportunity for us to get to know each other. We never get much time to be alone and just talk and communicate. Would that be something you're interested in?"

"Yeah, I guess we could get together and get to know each other better."

That's a go signal! When they got to the conference, she received a message in her room to call him. She did, and he said, "It's the first night of the conference. How would you like to go to dinner?"

She said, "Fine. I'm hungry. We could go for dinner."

And he said, "Well, what would you like to do? We could go to the restaurant here in the hotel, but we'd probably run into people we know and get interrupted. Or we could go to a quiet place where we could be private and alone and really get to know each other. I'd prefer the quiet restaurant."

"Fine," she replied.

Another go message! So they end up in the restaurant, and now they are talking and eating dinner. During dessert he reaches out across the table and touches her hand.

She just leaves it there, so he begins holding her forearm. Then he announces, "It really feels good being with you," and he squeezes her hand.

She squeezes back, saying, "It's really good to be with you, too. It was a pleasant dinner." Here's another go message.

He takes the check and they go outside, where he says, "You know, it's a warm night. This is a very nice restaurant with nice grounds. Do you want to go back to the hotel or would you like to go for a walk around the grounds? There's a beautiful moon."

She replies, "What do you want to do?"

"I'd like to take a walk." So as they start walking he goes from the arm to the forearm, to the hand, to the arm around the shoulder, to the arm around the waist. The arm creeps down and they're walking hand in hand and talking. At this point, she *still* says that she didn't believe anything was going on.

"He's been a friend for twelve years," she tells me. "He couldn't be flirting with me." What an insult to this guy! Because he's a friend, he checks his sex at the door?

So they drive back to the hotel, where he says, "I have some soft drinks in my room. Would you like to come up, and we can finish our conversation?"

"Sure, I'm thirsty," she says. They go up to his room, she sits down on his bed, and says, "Boy, my shoes are killing me. Mind if I take them off?"

"Not at all. In fact, mine hurt, too. Mind if I take mine off?" He also takes off his coat and loosens his tie. He fixes two drinks, pulls the chair up next to the bed, and hands her a drink. They sit and talk for a moment, and then he leans over and *all of a sudden for no reason at all* he kisses her! At which point she freaks out, pushes him away, accuses him of being a horrible monster, and storms out of the room.

She was lucky this guy was a mature human being who wasn't drunk at the time, because she was at high risk of date rape.

There is no excuse for a male to ever force himself sexually on a woman against her will. That is illegal, immoral, and unacceptable. Any man who believes that because he is turned on in the context of being with a woman—that that gives him some right to act out sexually with her against her will—is someone who needs therapy or a jail cell.

Date Rape

Women are often victims of date rape. Although the causes of date rape are complex, there are two fundamental principles that apply: (1) Women are not responsible for the sexual aggression of men. Men are responsible for their own behavior. In an ideal world, all men would be sensitive to the needs of women and would not act in a sexually aggressive manner. (2) This is *not* an ideal world and women are often victimized by men who have not learned how to deal appropriately with their sexual urges and aggression.

There is an unfortunate rule that says, "The victim beware." It warns that the person who is most often victimized is the one who needs to take the most precautions. We may not like this, but it is a reality. If women, especially single women in dating situations, do not take adequate precautions to protect themselves from sexual aggression, they are likely to be victimized.

As men begin to raise their consciousness and as they start taking more responsibility for their sexual behavior, circumstances will change. In my experience, however, the men who need this consciousness-raising the most are the ones who are the least likely to seek help. They are unwilling to get involved in education and counseling that will change their attitudes and beliefs about women and themselves. And it is this that causes the sexual aggression. Generally, the men who come to workshops on relationships and personal growth are those who are the least likely to be sexually aggressive.

For women to protect themselves sexually, they need to become an expert at identifying the progression from attraction to flirtation to sensuality to sexuality. They need to understand the sexual signals that men send to them and the signals that they send in response. If you don't want to escalate to the next step of a sexual relationship, give a very clear and nonambiguous "no" message at the earliest opportunity. It must be verbally stated and reinforced with body language.

Women place themselves at high risk of date rape when they inadvertently give go signals during the flirtation process. Men who are most prone to sexual aggression have male ego problems. Once they believe a woman is interested in them, it often becomes an issue of personal male identity to be able to sexually conquer her. Therefore, it is important to set the boundaries early on in flirtation and to be sure certain safety factors are built in.

Here are some guidelines:

1. The likelihood of a man becoming sexually aggressive is greatly heightened when he is under the influence of alcohol. Research shows that as little as two or three drinks can double his aggression. Do not put yourself in high-risk romantic situations or be alone with a man who has been drinking unless you are comfortable with him sexually and intend to follow through.

2. Most men who become sexually aggressive have serious therapy issues that they have never dealt with. These issues are not obvious. It is important to screen prospective partners before you put yourself in vulnerable situations with them. It is also important to recognize that no matter how carefully you screen someone, there is no substitute for in-depth knowledge about a person through experience.

3. If you want to avoid sexual aggression, play it safe. If you're dating and a man has more than two drinks, don't be alone with him. The biggest excuse men use for sexual aggression is that they were too drunk to know what they were doing. Drinking, drug use, and sexual aggression go hand in hand. If a man gets drunk and you're on a date, leave. If someone gets drunk with you in a dating situation, it's due to one of three reasons. Either he doesn't care about you, he believes it's a good time to get drunk, or he's an alcoholic who can't control his drinking behavior. Any one of those three reasons is

enough to give a rational person reasons to think about whether or not to move on to the next step of a relationship.

Once women understand the warning signals and how to protect themselves from sexual aggression, they can proceed with learning how to build relationships with a higher level of security and peace of mind. As sexual aggression and appropriate respect for the rights of women in sexual situations is acknowledged, this will become less of a concern for all involved.

We're building some bridges. First of all, you can control your attractions because you can turn on or shut off quickly. If you feel an attraction, you can embrace it, play with it, and do anything you want with it, and you can shut it down before you act on it and give any signals to anybody about it. But if you choose to, you can turn the attraction into flirtation, begin putting out subtle feelers, and see if the other person feels the same way.

Gender Affirmation

Flirtation is a process of gender affirmation. It's the process whereby one person tells another, "I find you attractive!" We all need gender affirmation. We crave it and we look for it. Unfortunately, most people think it's bad when it's not. And most people do it without acknowledging it; as a result, they don't take responsibility for it or set limits on it.

Most fun flirtation occurs when the vibes are going and there's very low-level physical contact. The sparks are flying and it's a really neat experience. But now, if it's going to move into sensuality, if it starts getting into some serious physical affection, like sexual hugging and kissing, you had better take it from the nonverbal to the verbal level. You need to say, "Hey, are you flirting with me?" Or if you want to take more responsibility, you can say, "I'm flirting with you and this is feeling really neat. How about you? Are you flirting back?"

But there is also a fear here. Typically, there is some horrendous vision of what's going to happen if you do this, like the person is going to be offended. But actually, an incredible sexual charge will permeate the relationship right then and there. And this doesn't mean you have to move all the way to sensuality. If the person says, "I wasn't flirting with you. As a matter of fact, if you're flirting with me, I think you should stop it." This hurts, but you know where you stand and can renegotiate your expectations of the relationship at that point.

But if your partner is also flirting with you, then you can raise the next issue by saying, "What are we going to do about this? Let's talk about it." Or you might be more comfortable saying, "I'm not sure what I want to do with this. I'm attracted to you, but I want to let you know that I'm committed elsewhere, and this would complicate my life." Here, you know what the limits are. "Yes, I'm attracted to you, and there's a part of me that would love to act out on it, but I'm not going to do it right now because it's not a good thing for me. So if we go on flirting, don't believe it's going to go anywhere because I'm not going to let it."

Another option is to say, "I don't know where I want this to go. The attraction is here, and part of me wants to act on it and part of me doesn't." And the third extreme is, "I know exactly what I want to do and where I want to go with this. I would like to be alone with you so we can make love."

Sexuality

Verbal negotiations should occur before heavy sensuality begins. Then when you get into sensuality in a big way—heavy necking, petting, and exchanges of physical affection—you don't have to go to the next level which is sexuality. One or both partners has the right to put a limit on it and say, "No, we need to stop here." But if you haven't talked about it beforehand, it's very difficult to put on the brakes.

In this day of AIDS, sensuality is getting a lot more prominent in sexual relations than is actual intercourse because you can get all of the neat feelings of arousal without the risk of disease transmission. But you have to be pretty mature about your sexual attitudes to be able to accept that. It's okay to do heavy necking or petting and even stimulate your partner to an orgasm without actually risking intercourse. It's perfectly fine, and more and more people are doing that. They're learning the secrets of sexual gratification without taking it all the way to sexual intercourse or oral sexuality.

This is a different way of thinking about it. The fantasy of being swept off your feet while turtledoves fly gracefully overhead is what you have to give up if you want to have a conscious, healthy relationship. Conscious relationships are based on choices, not fantasies.

You can engage in this four-step process of attraction, flirtation, sensuality, and sexuality without even knowing who your partner is. You can be attracted to someone, flirt with them, move into sensuality and find it mutually exciting, then go into a full sexual encounter and not even know the person's name. That's neither right nor wrong. I don't care what consenting adults do as long as both partners are honest and up front about what they are doing. I am not a moral judge. This brief encounter has been named by numerous experts. I call it recreational sex. The problem is, you can't have pure recreational sex without any of the platonic attachments. All sex carries with it some kind of interpersonal strings. When you have sex with somebody else, you never know what the emotional aftermath is going to be for you. You might fall in love with the person. He or she might *not* fall in love with you. It's risk-taking.

Romantic Love

You cannot make the leap from erotic sexuality to romantic love unless you have moved into the level of a friendship on the platonic scale. You can have sex with someone who is not a friend, but you can't make love to somebody who's not a friend. Making love implies an honest interchange between two people who know each other thoroughly.

The most satisfying sexual relationships occur between sexual friends, friends who are also sexually attracted to each other. Now it's a little different experience than picking up somebody in a bar who's a little dangerous, or having sex with a stranger in a hotel room. That gives you a different kind of a rush which some people interpret as pleasant, but it's not romantic love. Romantic love implies that you've been through an acquaintanceship stage, a companionship, and there's at least a developing of a friendship where you know the person you're with thoroughly, and you prefer to be with them.

Committed Love

Once romantic love has occurred, you can move to committed love. Here, you decide that this person is special enough to you, that you care about this person enough to make a commitment to meet his or her sexual and romantic needs as best you can, while he or she does the same for you. Then you agree to eliminate other sexual and romantic partners. That's committed love.

Family

The final level is family, where you decide that you love each other so much that you want to reproduce yourself by having and raising children. You not only physically recreate yourself but also recreate the love and the values that you share with your partner.

And that's ideally what a family should be. It's a conscious choice to recreate the highest values that are shared between two love partners and to create children who are capable of sharing and taking those values to even higher levels than you could. Unfortunately, that's not always how this works out.

Pathways to Love

There are different pathways to love. The first thing I'm going to explain is the pathway prescribed by the old courtship rituals. The rules started breaking down in the late 1960s. They were never made explicit, but here's my interpretation.

Platonically, you were an acquaintance of somebody to whom you were sexually attracted. You were allowed to feel attracted and to honor that attraction by flirting. You could get into verbal flirtation and low-level physical contact, but that was it. You could hold hands, but you couldn't kiss. A peck on the cheek good night was all that was allowed.

Then when the person cared enough about you to invite you into a companionship, when you shared enough activities that things started making sense and feeling good, you were allowed to get into sensuality. You could neck and pet.

After the companionship built, you were allowed progressive levels of sensuality. You restricted sexuality and romantic love to the point where a friendship developed. So you only had sex with friends. That's the ultimate rule I try to teach people: *Don't ever have sex with a stranger.* If that one simple rule were only honored universally, you could save yourself a lot of grief.

The fourth level, of course, is partnership, and this leads to committed love and family. I believe there's a high level of responsibility on the part of both partners to make sure children are not brought into a relationship accidentally. When children are brought in accidentally and are not wanted, they typically are not parented well. As a result, they never learn how to love and be intimate; as they grow up they contribute to society's problems instead of society's solutions. Children should be a result of conscious, loving choices, and as a conscious society we need to teach our children how to make conscious choices.

Choices

In the 1990s, there's very little excuse for accidental pregnancy. There's huge controversy over the issue of abortion, although people are missing the whole point. If we were a society that was sexually liberated enough to openly and honestly teach our ourselves and our children how to use the available birth control technology and to take responsibility for not having a family until they were in a committed relationship with a person they loved, we wouldn't have to deal with the abortion issue. But I don't hear anybody talking about that. It's the sexually repressive nature of this society—the closed system of talking about sexuality and contraception—that is creating these problems in the first place.

Other Pathways

There are three other pathways to building relationships. One pathway is to build a relationship backwards. Sometimes it works and sometimes it doesn't. This occurs when you meet someone, are powerfully attracted to them, begin to flirt, get sensually involved, lose your head, become sexually involved, and say, "What have I done? That was really neat, but I don't even know this person." So then you back up and decide to get to know each other, develop a companionship and a friendship, decide you like each other, and then build a partnership that leads to committed love. That's the sexual pathway into relationships. It happens a lot; about one-third of relationships start that way. About a third of those relationships grow into long-term love relationships. The final third of the relationships start out as acquaintances with little or no sexual attraction. They become companions, and as they get to know each other on an in-depth basis, the sexuality turns on, the attraction begins, and then they go through the continuum of sexual behaviors.

None of these pathways is either right or wrong as far as I'm concerned. The point is if you want to have effective human relationships, you have to become responsible choicemakers. You can choose how you're going to build your relationships. You can take it through a sexual channel and then backtrack and build the platonic. The risk involves getting into sexuality with a partner and then finding you have nothing in common. Little substance and the relationship is going to go nowhere. It's not necessarily bad. You may have had a neat short-term experience. Or you can say you're going to get a solid friendship before you let anyone flirt with you. Again, it's not bad, but a lot of potentially viable partners are not willing to wait six months to a year to kiss you good night.

I have many people who misunderstand me and say, "Well, I'm working on building a friendship, but I feel it's got to be ten months to a year before I know a person well enough to be friends. They should be patient enough to wait." It's not likely that it's going to happen that way. Or you can build a relationship in stages. All of those are viable choices, and they're choices that are up to you.

Skills

Knowledge alone isn't going to help you to build a healthy relationship. There are skill-building steps to each of the levels. You need to develop acquaintanceship skills. How do you get into warm, cordial, superficial, friendly relationships with people? You need to accept that you can have acquaintanceships without them needing to go anywhere. You need companionship skills. How do you find preferred activities, learn how to invite and be invited by other people to share activities? How do you develop a friendship? How do you commit to another person as a friend, in a way that you can enjoy their company, support them, listen to them, understand them, take them seriously, affirm them as people, and be there for them without losing your personhood in them? How do you negotiate an agreement where they reciprocate the same benefit for you? And how do you become partners? How do you go about establishing conscious agreements and commitments when it pertains to serious aspects of your life?

These are all skills. So is the area of attraction—learning how to get in touch with your sexual attraction patterns and how to change those patterns if you're only attracted to people who cannot or will not meet your needs. Flirtation is a skill. It's not something that magically happens. You have to learn how to do it. Then recognize when it's being done to you so you can choose whether to respond to it or stop.

Sensuality involves skills. How do you caress, touch, and embrace another human being in a way that is pleasant for them and pleasant for you? Sexuality is a skill. How do you learn how to do sexual pleasuring with your partner? How do you learn your own turn-ons, and how do you tell your partner so he or she can do the things that turn you on? And how can you take an interest in your partner's turn-ons and learn how to do the things that turn him or her on? That's what sexuality is all about.

Romantic love is a skill. How can you combine friendship and all the intimacy of friendship with the intimacy of sexuality and stop having sex and start making love? Love, on a romantic basis, is an intimate sharing. It's a spiritual experience where the personhoods of two people merge together. There's a spiritual bonding. And then how do you make a decision to commit? How do you make little commitments and build to bigger and bigger ones until you're willing to commit to somebody one day at a time? And then how do you make the decision about family? How do you decide whether or not to have children? Those are the skill areas you need to deal with. If you come from a dysfunctional family, you probably never learned about any of it except on television and by watching how your parents did it.

So when you fall in love and go on unconscious automatic pilot, you start recreating your childhood in your adult love relationships. So remember, first the self. You've got to heal yourself and get a life that's yours. Then you can move into the area of relationship.

The Process of Communicating

To make it in a relationship, you must learn how to communicate intimately with your partner. It is an important skill.

In 1969 I learned how to do communications training with couples as part of my family therapy training. As recently as two years ago, I went through an extended ten-day workshop with Harvelle Hendrix who has a technique he calls, "The couple's dialogue." It's outlined in his best-selling book, *Getting the Love You Want.* I integrated a lot of what I learned from his experience into the model that I currently use to teach patients.

In order to communicate, you need to get some understanding of yourself and some understanding of how to share yourself. People need to identify, within themselves, these three levels of personal self-disclosure.

The Three Levels of Self-Disclosure

The first level of self-disclosure is the *public self,* which consists of general knowledge that is used with acquaintances and companions. It's nice, safe stuff that nobody can use to hurt you. When I talk to an audience, I'm at the public-self level. There's no way I will disclose things about myself that are embarrassing or that somebody can use to blackmail me or hurt me. I will not share unfinished business. I will share a lot of things about myself, but if something is very uncomfortable for me, I will not talk about it in front of a large audience. I honor myself more than that. And I don't put myself at risk lightly. If I'm going to put myself at risk, it will be for an important cause.

The second level of self-disclosure is the *private self*, which holds sensitive issues, issues that you discuss with friends, lovers, and therapists. These are unresolved issues, unfinished business, things that have the capability of causing you pain, things that you reserve. You don't usually talk about them with total strangers, because when you talk about them, you do so at risk of emotional pain. You choose to make yourself vulnerable.

The third level of self-disclosure is the *intimate self,* which involves intense personal sharing in the present tense. It's used with close friends and lovers. Many people confuse the private self and the intimate self.

I know many people who are in recovery, a lot of them therapists, who believe that the hallmark of intense intimacy is to sit naked in bed with a lover talking about how much you hurt because of your family of origin. That isn't what this is all about. Neither is sitting around intimately with your partner talking about your personal pain and your pain pockets. That kind of stuff goes on in intimate relationships, but it's not the hallmark or the essence of intimacy.

Communicating at Any Level

No matter what level you communicate on, you're going to need to organize yourself in such a way that you can talk about four different things. The first thing you need to do at any level of communication is to tell your partner what you are thinking. "What I'm thinking is...."

The second area of what's communicated is feeling. "What I'm feeling is...."

The third area that's communicated is actions or behaviors. "What I am doing or what I have an urge to do is...." And when you talk about behaviors, it's very important to talk about two things. "What I'm going to do about it is...." and, "What I'd like to do about it if I thought I could get away with it is...." Very often we have urges to do things that we wouldn't actually do.

Then the fourth level is motivation. What is causing me to think, feel, and act this way? What is the motivation behind it? Where does it come from? "My motivation is...."

Usually, when we get into conflict with our intimate relationships, we believe that 99 percent of the conflict has to do with the here-and-now issue. In some situations less than 20 percent of it has to do with the here-and-now issue, and 80 percent of it is unfinished business that both partners drag up from the past and dump on each other.

Unfinished Business

Here's a scenario. You're late coming home from work by ten minutes. The last time I was with an intimate partner who was late, she was having an affair on me, and I've never forgiven her for it. Now you are ten minutes late for the first time in your whole life and you walk into the door straight into a buzz saw.

"Wait a minute," you say. "I got stuck in traffic, what's the big deal?"

"Huh," I reply. "You would say that. All people are that way."

My reaction has very little to do with my partner, and it has a great deal to do with my unfinished business. This unfinished business gets tapped powerfully in intimate relationships. It helps to know where this stuff is coming from, what our motivations are.

The Public Self

Here's an example of public-self communication. I meet somebody and I say, "Hi, How are you? I'm Terry." And you say, "Hi, I'm Mary." Then I say, "You know, what I'm thinking right now is that we might have something in common to talk about. I'm a therapist in Chicago and attending this workshop. I'm feeling really interested in you and kind of attracted to you as well. I'd like to get to know you better. That's what I'd like to do." That's a safe communication. I'm interested. I'd like to get to know you better. I think we might have some things in common because we're sharing the workshop.

Or if you're talking to a friend, you say, "Hey, did you read in the paper that we're back in Iraq again, and we're thinking about going back to war because Saddam Hussein has some nuclear weapons? I'm feeling angry and outraged about this because we spent all this money on a war we never finished. And what I'd like to do about it is help bring about a change in the White House." Now that's very acceptable public-self kind of sharing.

The Private and Intimate Selves

When you move into the private self, you start talking about personal issues. And when you move into the intimate self, the key is immediacy. The key is right now. "What I am thinking about you right now is.... What I am feeling about you right now is.... And what you stir or arouse in me, what I'd like to do with you right now is...."

Here's an example of how this works. You're with a lover, and you look him right in the eye and say, "What I'm thinking about you right now is that you're very attractive. Your eyes are very appealing to me, and it's very important that I'm with you right now. I'm feeling very warm inside. I'm feeling very attracted and turned on to you right now. And what I'd like to do is give you a gigantic hug. I'd just like to forget about everything and just hug you and roll around on the bed with you right now."

Feel the power of that. That's the kind of intimate interaction and communication that I'm talking about. There are other kinds where you move into the sharing of your private self, talking about your pain and your unresolved issues, but I strongly recommend that you separate your intimate lovemaking from your discussion of your unresolved personal problems. Don't bring your pain and problems into bed with you.

Four Areas of Communication

There are four areas of communication: reading, writing, talking, and listening. In school we received the most training in reading, then writing, and then talking. Very few of us ever took a course in listening. So we end up with one verbal skill where we've had some training, and one where we've had virtually none. Most people talk and don't listen. They have mutually timed monologues.

The Couple's Dialogue

Here is a dialogue procedure that is a modification of a procedure I learned from Harvelle Hendrix. I have operationalized it in a way that I am more comfortable with, and before I tell you the seven steps in detail, I'm going to tell you the simplest way to communicate with another human being.

Communication consists basically of four steps. Step number one is, I self-disclose to you. I tell you what I'm thinking, what I'm feeling, and what I have an urge to do about it. And perhaps I tell you about my motivations, about what is stirring that up.

In step two, you listen to me, understand me, take me seriously, and affirm what I am saying. There are skills—self-disclosure (I self-disclose to you) and listening (you listen and give me feedback that affirms me).

In step three the roles switch. You self-disclose to me. In step four I listen and give you feedback that affirms you.

In its simplest terms, this is intimate communication. I talk, you listen, you respond and affirm that you have heard what I have said, and then you talk, I listen, and I affirm that I have heard what you have said. It's really just that simple. But it's difficult to do it if you have not been trained in communication.

Usually, when I talk you don't listen. You prepare what you're going to say, and as soon as I take a breath, you jump in and say it. During this time, I take a deep breath and prepare what I'm going to say. As a result, no one ever gets a sense that the other person is listening. So we're going to devise a procedure that will allow effective communication to occur between couples. Now this procedure is going to seem artificial at first, and people aren't going to like it. But once you start using it, once you learn the skill, you'll see that it helps a lot.

This procedure is used when you are talking about a serious, emotionally charged issue. You don't use it when you are just chatting with an acquaintance on the public-self level.

The Seven Steps of Intimate Communication

The first step is you prepare to self-disclose. The second step is you make an appointment with your partner to talk with her. The third step is you prepare to listen. The fourth step is self-disclosing: you tell your partner what you want to say. In the fifth step, your partner listens, using active listening to make sure that she heard. In the sixth step, she responds to you. Then you repeat steps three through six, reversing roles as many times as you need to bring the conversation to a closure. When you close the conversation, you affirm to each other what you've learned or what new understandings have emerged from the communication.

The Dented Car

Here's a fictitious example. I'm married and my wife's name is Jan. Let's imagine that I just bought a brand new car, the first new car I ever bought in my life. It's precious to me because when I was a little kid, I was the youngest in a family of six brothers. I would always get all the hand-me-downs and I'd never get anything new. Anytime I did get something new, one of my older brothers would steal it from me, play with it until it broke, and give it back to me.

Finally, for the first time in my life, I have a new car. I park it in the garage, and the fourth morning after I bought it I notice a dent on the driver's side door. Instantly, this huge feeling wells up inside me. I see the dent, and I immediately know who did it. It's parked right next to Jan's car, and she has the habit of putting groceries on the passenger side seat. In my mind, I know instantly that she opened the door and, as she was getting the groceries out, banged her car door into my car door. She dented my car and didn't tell me about it. She hoped I wouldn't notice it, that I'd take it to work and think it happened in the parking lot.

And I know this and am enraged. I feel such a huge sense of anger that I want to take my key and scratch her car in revenge—a terribly mature reaction.

So now, if I have no communications training, I storm right back into the house. As she's putting files into her briefcase, I say, "Jan, I am furious with you. You dented my car door and then lied to me about it."

She says, "Your car door is dented? What do you mean?"

"Well, you did it. You know what I mean."

"Look, Terry, I'd like to talk to you about this. I'm sorry it's dented. Is it real serious?"

"Well, no, it's not real serious."

"Good, then we can talk about it tonight. I'm late for work."

"No, Jan, we're going to talk about it now. I'm not going to put up with this from you. You always treat me as if I don't count. You never tell me that you care about me. I've got a problem, and we need to talk about it right now."

"Well, I've got to go to work. I've got an appointment in four minutes, and it takes me six minutes to get there. I love you and I care about you, but I can't talk to you about this now."

"Don't give me that bunk," I say. "If you loved me, you would talk to me right now. You don't love me. I don't know why I put up with this."

"Terry, you're being unreasonable. I don't know why I put up with you. I'll see you tonight." She storms out of the house, gets in her car, and drives away. Then I storm out of the house, get into my car, and drive away, too—and we *both* have miserable days. This is not effective communication. This is a sign of immature people who have never learned how to communicate. Now here's how to do it, following the communication formula.

Using the Communication Formula

As soon as I notice the car door and feel this emotion well up inside me, I need to stop before I react. If you want to communicate effectively, you have to learn to put a filter between your brain and your mouth. The inability to do this is called immaturity. This is the first objection I get whenever I tell couples about this.

"Do you mean I can't say exactly what I feel to my partner when I feel it?"

I say, "That's right."

"But what am I supposed to do with my feelings?"

"Manage them. Talk to a friend. Write them down. You're an adult. Children explode every time they have a feeling. Adults should be able to contain their feelings until it is appropriate to talk about them."

A mistaken belief about intimacy is that we should be able to emotionally vomit on our partners at will without them getting upset. This is a sign of relationship immaturity. Sometimes we treat our animals better than our partners. We have to recognize that our partners are human beings who deserve respect.

When I manage my feelings, I stop myself and acknowledge that I am really upset, I'm really angry. I ask myself, what is actually going on here? I have to sort out my thoughts. What am I thinking? Here's what I'm thinking. "My car is scratched. Jan did it. She's going to lie to me, and that's unacceptable. I don't want her to lie."

What am I feeling? "I feel angry and enraged!" Why am I so enraged? "Because she lied to me. It's not so much the car, it's the fact that she lied and tried to hide it." I've got this urge to scratch her car. That's not too healthy. That's the action, the urge. It tells me that something is wrong because I'm not the kind of guy who takes revenge like that. So then I ask, What's causing my reaction? Then I calm down and find myself flooded with the same kind of feelings I used to have when my older brother would break my toys.

So now I've got a sense of what's going on, and I can take a deep breath and calm down. And if to calm down I have to call a friend and talk to him first, I do so. People who love one another do not approach each other to initiate conversation while they are enraged.

Making an Appointment

My next step is to make an appointment. When I walk in and see Jan at the counter, I express a need by saying, "Jan, I have a need to talk to you." I express a level of communication. "This involves a very serious personal issue. My car is dented, and I want to talk to you about the damage. I'm upset about it, and it's really important. Can we schedule time now? When is the nearest time in the future that you can set up some time to meet with me? This is a hot issue, and it's very important and very serious to me."

Jan says, "Terry, I'd love to talk to you about it right now but I've got a client coming in less than ten minutes. Would it be possible for us to schedule it later? I'm going to be home between twelve and one for lunch. Can we do it then?"

"Well no, I've got clients at lunchtime. I can't do it then, but how about this evening. I'll be home at six."

"Well no, I'm not going to be home until eight. How about then?"

"That's fine." And we set up a time.

It's important to set up appointments because if I don't, her mind is somewhere else. I'm inviting her to discount me. I want her to schedule a time when I can be the number-one focus of her attention. She's got a busy life, and making me the center of her universe is not her job. If you believe that it is your partner's job to make you the center of her universe anytime you want, you should go into therapy to treat your out-of-control grandiosity. If you expect to be the center of her life, it's irrational and unreasonable. It's reasonable to expect that person to clear time to talk to you within twenty-four hours or the next day. It would be unacceptable if she says, "Yeah, I understand that this is very important. How about a week from next Thursday?" That's a direct message that she doesn't care. It's enough if she makes an effort to schedule you in at the earliest possible time.

Between now and then, you manage your feelings. You talk it through with a friend or recovery sponsor.

When we finally come together, the first thing we do when we start talking is set the stage. I say, "Jan, I've got something to talk about, and I'm not saying this to hurt you, but this is going to be a hot issue for me, so why don't you get ready to listen to me."

When you're going to listen, you need to go through a self-protection ritual. You protect yourself by reminding yourself not to overreact. It's like putting up a psychic shield to defend yourself against the other person.

So Jan prepares by first saying to herself, "Now, Terry's going to say something, and it's a hot issue for him. It's obvious that he's upset, but I don't have to let this emotionally affect me in a serious way. I can take a couple deep breaths and relax."

Then she needs to detach from herself by saying, "This is not about me. Terry's upset. It's my job to listen to what he has to say. I'm not here to meet my needs right now. I'm here to listen to him, to understand him."

Then she engages herself with me. "I'm here to listen to Terry, to try to understand what he is saying to me, to take him seriously so that he knows that I understand and care, and then to affirm his right to feel that way and his right to think that way—to tell him in essence that he's not crazy. That's my job."

I Self-Disclose

The next step is for me to self-disclose. I say, "Jan, I want to talk to you about the fact that as you were taking groceries out of the car yesterday, you slammed your car door into my car and put a dent in the door. You didn't tell me about it. You lied to me. I imagine you wanted me to drive to work and think that it was dented there. And I'm feeling really angry. I was so mad that I wanted to scratch your car in retaliation. That's what I had an urge to do, but I decided that I was going to talk to you about it and process this with you. My motivations are this. You know that I've told you about my family, especially my brothers who used to break all my stuff. You know how important this new car is to me. Then you put a dent in it and don't tell me, and I feel exactly like I used to feel when my brothers beat up on me. But I'm not going to let you beat up on me and break my stuff like my brothers did without protecting myself. Got it? Clear?"

"Very clear." So now it's her turn to actively listen. While I am talking, she is trying to understand what I'm thinking. So she does a mental checklist. Did he talk about his thoughts? If he did, am I clear on them? If not, she says, "I'm not clear on what you're thinking. Give me that again." If she's not clear on what I'm feeling, she probes for it. What is your partner doing or having an urge to do? She makes sure she's got it straight. And what is motivating him to think, feel, and act this way? Then, after the active listening, she responds to me.

In any intimate relationship, 70 to 80 percent of any problem is simply the need to have your partner hear and understand you. It's the need to become psychologically visible to your partner so that they hear what you are saying and respond to it. Most people don't realize this.

She Responds

The first thing Jan does is paraphrase my thoughts and say to me, "Well, Terry, I'm hearing you say that you believe I dented your car when I was taking the groceries out last night. You believe I lied to you about it, hoping you wouldn't notice it, and that you'd take it to work and think it happened at your parking lot. I hear that you're very angry with me, even enraged, and that you feel I'm treating you like your brothers used to treat you, and that you're not going to tolerate it. It sounds like something very powerful is being tapped inside of you. Have I got it?"

"Yea, I think so." I'm satisfied that she knows what I'm feeling. So then she validates it by saying, "Given the fact that you believe I dented your car, hid it from you and lied to you, and would put it off and blame it on somebody else, I can understand your thinking and feeling that way. I really can. Because if I believed that you broke something of mine and tried to hide it, I would be angry with you and have awful feelings about it also. And given what you believe about this situation, you're not crazy for thinking and feeling this way.

Wow, I think this is great. But we're not ready to move into closure yet. Now we go back. It's Jan's turn to say, "I heard you. Now I have something that I want to talk to you about. Is this a good time?"

"All right." So now I prepare to listen, to shift roles. I have been talking, which requires one mind-set, but now I have to clear my mind and get ready to take in new information. I start by protecting myself, thinking that I don't have to overreact to what Jan is going to say. Obviously I hit a raw nerve and she feels very guilty. She got caught doing something here. I've exposed her, but I love her and I care about her. She's going to feel awful; she's going to be trashing herself; she's going to be down on herself—but I don't have to take responsibility for all that pain. It's okay, she's a fallible human being, and I detach from myself because I'm not here right now to meet my needs. I'm here to help her with her pain, her sorrow, her regret, and her remorse. I'm here to listen to her, to understand her, to take her seriously, and to affirm her. Now that I have my psychic shield up I say, "All right, Jan, go to it."

She Self-Discloses

And she says, "Here's the issue. I didn't dent your car. I didn't buy groceries yesterday. I did not open the door on that side of the car. I'm sorry that your car is dented, but I didn't do it. And what I am thinking is how insensitive and insecure you are to assume that I did it without ever asking me. What I am wondering is why I am married to someone who thinks I'm a liar. If you think I would lie about something as trivial as a dent in your car door, how could you ever trust me with anything significant in our relationship? I am feeling angry, hurt, and like I ought to walk out of this relationship right now. You know that I was raised in a family where I was always the scapegoat. Anytime anything went wrong in my family, they blamed me. Because I was powerless over it, I suffered the most. I'm *not* going to take the same kind of crap from you, fella."

It didn't quite go the way I thought it would.

I Respond

So now it's my turn to paraphrase. Although I've got some stuff stirring around, I've got to be mature and remember that I'm not here to respond to my needs. She listened to me; now it's my turn. I say, "Huh. What I'm hearing you say is that you didn't dent my car. Is that right?"

"Yeah, that's right."

"You didn't even buy groceries yesterday—is that right?"

"Yes, that's right."

"You mean that my car got dented somewhere else?"

"Yeah, Terry, it did. Probably at work, *before* you got home, and you just didn't notice it."

"You're not lying to me?"

"I'm not lying to you."

"And I'm hearing you say that you're very angry with me for blaming you without even giving you the courtesy of asking you, that you're wondering why you're married to me if I think you're going to lie to me about a little thing like a dented car door, and how could I ever trust you with more important things. The credibility is short, and you're thinking why should you be married to someone who distrusts you. Is that right?"

She says, "Yes, it is."

"And I'm also hearing you say that this is being triggered because you were always the scapegoat in your family, and you don't want me scapegoating and blaming you anymore. Is that right?"

"Yeah, that's right."

Now this next step really hurts, but I've got to say, "You know, it makes sense to me that if you didn't dent my car, that you'd think this way. And if I do get this upset, and if I do think you could be dishonest over this little thing, then we do have serious trouble in our relationship. It makes sense that you're thinking and feeling that way. You're not crazy for doing it. Did I get that right?"

"Yeah."

So now I respond. We're not ready for closure yet because we have to go back again. I have to say, "Jan, I've got something else to say to you. Would you get ready to listen." This is a very important little ritual because it allows the person to shift gears and attend to you. When you're self-disclosing, you're in one gear and have to give your partner time to change, making the role explicit.

She puts up her psychic shield. She's ready to listen, reminding herself that she doesn't have to overreact to what I'm saying.

I say, "Jan, the issue is I was wrong. I realize, now that I think about it, the car could have been dented at work. I believe you that you didn't dent it, and I can see how I instantly went into my blaming reflex. My blaming reflex got activated and went out of control. It was unfair of me to blame you, and I can see that what I'm feeling right now is scared and guilty. I'm thinking that I've been unfair. What I've got an urge to do is just apologize because I really don't want our relationship to end or be damaged because of something as insignificant as a dent on the car door. I can get it fixed, so that's not the big deal there. The big deal is I thought you were lying to me, and I can see now that you weren't And I feel terrible. What's causing me to feel this way is that I love you and I care about you. I value our relationship and hate to see it damaged by something like this."

Now it's Jan's turn again. She tries to understand and paraphrases, "What I'm hearing you say is that you love and care about me, that you realize you were wrong."

I say, "That's right."

"And you're feeling kind of guilty and sad and scared. You're afraid that I'm going to leave."

"Yeah, that's right."

"And I'm also hearing you say that you value our relationship, you love me, you care about me, and you don't want the relationship to be damaged over something as trivial as a car door."

"Yeah, that's very right."

"Well, Terry, it makes sense to me that you are thinking and feeling this way because I am a worthwhile person. We do have a valuable relationship. We are both bigger than these kinds of little issues. And we should be able to survive these things. It makes perfect sense that you would think and feel this way after what you did."

Once again, we go back, and it is Jan's turn to say, "Terry, I've got something to say to you. Are you ready to listen?"

I prepare to listen by shifting gears from my talker to my listener mode. Then she says, "Terry, I just want to let you know the issue is that I love and care about you also. I realize I overreacted when you accused me of this. It does make me angry when you blame me, but I really added a lot of charge to that which I didn't need to add. What I am thinking is that I don't want a car door to ruin our relationship either, and I realize that you're working on the blaming stuff. Neither of us is perfect. I love you, I care about you, and I've got an urge to say, let's do what we have to do to put this thing behind us. My motivation is that I also think we have a valuable relationship, and I want to resolve this and put it behind us."

It's my turn to actively listen and say, "Well, Jan, what I'm hearing you say is that you think our relationship is really valuable, that we can get beyond this, and that you're not going to leave because you love me. Is that right?"

"Well, yeah."

"And it makes sense to me that you feel this way because I think we've got something really good here, too."

Closure

By this time we hug each other, and we move into closure by stating the new awareness. Each of us takes a turn.

I say, "You know, Jan, in the dialogue, I learned that I've got to control my blaming reflex. I've got it big time, and I realize it's not fair to you. That's an issue I have to work on. But I'd like to request for you to do something. Just give me the assurance—and it may be crazy but I need a commitment from you—that if you ever do break or damage anything of mine, that you will tell me before I accidentally find it. Realize this is a hot-button issue for me. I realize you may accidentally break something, so please let me know about it, especially when it pertains to this new car, which is a big deal. Did you hear what I asked for and are you willing to do it?"

And she says, "Well, yeah. I'm hearing you say that you learned about your blame reflex, and what you want me to do is tell you if I ever break anything. I'm willing to do that. But what I learned about this conversation is that I really have a hot button about being blamed. I've known it before, and even though it's not fair of you to blame me, I shouldn't react with wanting to trash the relationship. I'm going to work on my blame issues, but I want to request something of you, Terry. Before you make up your mind that I did something, ask me first. Before you judge me as guilty in your mind, ask me if I did it and give me a chance to respond. I'm going to have to insist on this. Did you hear what I said?"

"Yes. You're going to work on overreacting to the blame, but you're still not going to tolerate my blaming you unfairly. What you want me to do is check out whether or not you did it and only blame you for things that you really did."

"You got it."

And now we're finished with the dialogue.

When you're dealing with intimate communication, it's important to realize that some of the motivation and urges to act are caused by the current issue, but a whole bunch of them are caused by unfinished business and unresolved relationship issues. Today, you are finishing the fight you had yesterday. You're carrying over the anger and resentment from some issue you didn't resolve yesterday, and you're putting that charge onto a new issue. It can be unfinished past adult experiences, particularly unfinished relationships with other people. You're taking out your anger and rage at your previous partner on your current partner. Or they can come from unfinished childhood experiences where you are taking out that particular anger, rage, and hurt. This process allows you to put it all into perspective, and I recommend that couples use it.

Summary

The first thing I want to point out is this: *Relationships are not easy.* Every adult struggles with relationships even if you come from a healthy, functional family. Relationships are difficult because we are living in a society that is undergoing rapid and, at times, chaotic changes. The very nature of how men define themselves as men and how women define themselves as women is evolving. Our social fabric and what we expect from a relationship is changing.

Fifty years ago no sane person expected long-term sexual gratification in a relationship. People got married to form a financial unit and to raise children, not for hot sex. And if you went to court fifty years ago for a divorce and said, "Everything was fine in the relationship. My husband supports me, doesn't beat me, doesn't abuse me, doesn't cheat on me, but our sex life isn't satisfying and I believe it's irreconcilable, and we want to get a divorce," the judge would say, "I'm sorry, grow up. Marriage is not for sexual gratification."

Relationships are difficult. There's a lot of struggle and pain in dealing with relationships. I don't minimize the pain, but I also believe it's important that we not get hypnotized by it. When you are hurt, you need to acknowledge that you're in pain. You need to be able to talk about it, but you need to do what you need to do despite the pain. Many people make the mistake of saying they'll change it when they stop hurting. But they won't stop hurting until they change it.

Being in a dysfunctional relationship is like having a thorn in your foot. Every time you take a step, it hurts. Once you know the pain is caused by the thorn, you have a choice. You can reach down and yank that thorn out. Although it's going to hurt very badly for a little while, it will start to heal. But if you want to avoid the intense pain, it's going to get worse until it gets infected. If you still don't do anything, your foot is going to get gangrene and you'll need to have it amputated or you'll die. Now that is the analogy of a troubled relationship. You have to have the courage to face the pain and consciously renegotiate the relationship. If you can't renegotiate, you may have to leave. And it's going to hurt but pain heals.

If you wait until you're not hurting, you're never going to do anything.

If you want to find a relationship in which you will never hurt, give up. If you're going to be in love, you are going to hurt. It's part of the game. In love and intimacy, you give someone the power to hurt you—we are all fallible human beings, at best. If you open up your pain pockets, your partner is going to accidentally poke you from time to time. If you're a mature adult, if you've learned how to resolve your family-of-origin issues, you can deal with the pain. If the person keeps poking you in your pain pockets, you can set limits and stop them.

You can learn to take care of yourself. The goal in life is not to avoid pain. The goal is to live according to your values and experience the joy and the sorrow, the pain and the pleasure that goes along with that. All of those are part of the experience.

Everybody who makes a decision to love will ultimately get hurt. Ernest Hemingway said it this way. "All true stories end in death." That's the best you can hope for from an intimate relationship in the long run, that you'll both die together on the same night in your sleep. In reality, you either abandon your partner by dying first or your partner abandons you. If you don't come to terms with the fact you're going to die and spend your whole life avoiding the eminence of your death, you're never going to live.

You must come to terms with the reality that all love is transient, all love is temporary, all love is to be enjoyed for what it is in the moment. There are no guarantees that it's going to last or that it's going to be there tomorrow. Unless you can accept that, and you're willing to pay the price of that ultimate separation and ending, you will never have the courage to love. Love takes courage because it means you have to be willing to place the value you have for yourself on another person. And you must do that with the full knowledge that your partner is a fallible, mortal human being who may violate that trust periodically and who will eventually one day die.

A love relationship is not a romantic ideal. It doesn't take away the human condition. It doesn't protect us from death, anger, despair, or poverty. A relationship gives us a partner. It doesn't really solve or change anything. When we have a loving partner, we have a loving partner. If you're incompetent at dealing with your life and you have a loving partner, then you're going to be in love while being incompetent at dealing with your life. If you're sixty pounds overweight and you fall in love, then you're a sixty-pound overweight person who's in love. *Relationships don't fix anything.* They give us a supportive partner to help us deal with the rest of our lives. They don't do anything for you. They don't magically change anything. Your life doesn't magically transform.

There is no such thing as a perfect partner or the perfect relationship. All people are fallible and periodically have problems because all relationships are imperfect. There is no magic in a relationship. What you can find in the loving, the sharing, and the caring is a partner. In moments of intimacy, you can find a sense of comfort and support, nurturing and safety, with someone who cares about you and would never deliberately hurt you. Over time you can build and explore a whole different dimension of intimacy that integrates passion and safety in the same relationship.

I wish you all success in learning how to get love right!

Other recommended titles:

ADDICTIVE RELATIONSHIPS
Why Love Goes Wrong in Recovery
by Terence T. Gorski
Audiotape 17-0156-8

GETTING LOVE RIGHT
Learning the Choices of Healthy Intimacy
by Terence T.Gorski
Book 52-2901-4

GETTING LOVE RIGHT
Videotapes:
Tape I: Personal Growth for Healthy Intimacy
55-0948-3
Tape 2: Partner Selection
55-0949-1
Tape 3: Relationship Building
55-0950-5

Set of three videotapes:
55-0951-3

Audiotapes:
Tape I: Pesonal Growth for Healthy Intimacy
55-0952-1
Tape 2: Partner Selection
55-0954-8
Tape 3: Relationship Building
55-0955-6

Set of three audiotapes:
55-0956-4

THE PLAYERS AND THEIR PERSONALITIES
Understanding People Who Get Involved in Addictive Relationships
by Terence T. Gorski
17-0180-0

1-800-767-8181 816/252-5010